Adjusting to the New World Economy

Adjusting to the New World Economy

Michael R. Czinkota

BUSINESS EXPERT PRESS

Leader in applied, concise business books

Adjusting to the New World Economy

First published in 2022 by
Business Expert Press, LLC
222 East 46th Street, New York, NY 10017
www.businessexpertpress.com

ISBN-13: 978-1-63742-193-2 (paperback)
ISBN-13: 978-1-63742-194-9 (e-book)

Business Expert Press International Business Collection

First edition: 2022

10 9 8 7 6 5 4 3 2 1

For Ilona, Margaret, and Thomas, thank you for our many discussions that have led to new insights.

Description

Professor Czinkota shares with us his practical insights into the modern world trading system and the complexities that exist within. He provides an invaluable framework for future global leaders in their endeavors to solve global trade crises and find opportunities for furthering the flow of goods, services, and investment across borders.

It is rare to find such practical insights into the rationale of why the world is what it is today and makes for interesting guidance for the future. Anyone who reads this book will be better equipped to tackle the challenges of operating in the world economy and working their way out of conflicts.

The book also addresses the weaknesses present in current world structures, such as the World Trade Organization and its inability to suppress China, guiding the reader on how to achieve business success in a world of instability and diplomatic tensions. The concept of Curative International Marketing is a unique framework fathered by Professor Czinkota and is deeply explored in this book.

Keywords

international marketing; policy making; cultural interactions; curative marketing; technological relationships

Contents

Foreword

During the second term of President Ronald Reagan, I was the United States Department of Commerce Assistant Secretary for Trade Administration. Subsequently, I became Under Secretary of Commerce. In those positions, I had responsibility for regulating international trade and overseeing the defense industrial base. Those positions also provided me with the privilege of working with Michael Czinkota on a daily basis.

I was indeed fortunate. He was a valued member of my management team, and I relied on him for advice and counsel. All government officials are not equal in their skill and acumen. Michael Czinkota was one who was exceptional. He was particularly valuable to have as a colleague. I appreciated his insights into the practical workings of international trade and the interconnectedness of the modern trading system.

Reflecting that knowledge, in this book he shares some of his understanding of how the system functions, what aspects of trade are organic and inherent in the process of trading, and what are the strengths and weaknesses of the structures that have been created to bring order to the system and how to market into that environment. As he illustrates, language, culture, technology, proximity, and many other factors play a role in the success or failure of efforts to sell in the international environment.

As a former colleague, I attest to the accuracy with which he describes the factors which made up our decisions. In this book, through vivid illustrations and anecdotes, he analyzes the key factors that determine success or failure of international enterprises. These factors can require governmental action or signal a need for the government to get out of the way and allow private entrepreneurs themselves create a solution to the problem.

All too often, we hear government officials talk as though the United States is self-sufficient to control its actions and policies independent of its trading partners or the state of the world economy. These same individuals talk as though supply chains and joint ventures can be altered to fit the preferences of the president or the policy goals of any administration without regard to the preferences of our trading partners, or adversaries for that matter. These same individuals seem to be ignorant—or perhaps do not care—about how difficult it is to establish a reliable supply chain and how difficult it is to try to re-establish a supply chain or trade relationship if it is disrupted by government sanctions or changes in the technical parameters of export controls. Some, including both the current and former presidents, talk as though United States Government officials can increase exports with the snap of a finger, or bring industries back on shore when it suits the needs of our country.

Unfortunately, as one reads Dr. Czinkota's book, it will become clear that increasing exports or inducing companies to relocate in the continental United States involves a difficult and painstaking effort and does not always work out as planned, no matter how good the intentions. As he points out, over the past two years we have imposed tariffs on two-thirds of Chinese exports, and apparently what that has accomplished is to push the manufacturing of those products to other Asian countries, particularly Vietnam. It is a great aid program for Vietnam but not what we intended. The Chinese have suffered but so have we.

Dr. Czinkota demonstrates how interdependent and fluid world trade is. His data and insights give the reader an interesting and realistic perspective on international trade and marketing, a perspective that should help any policy maker or serious student of the subject understand just how complex trade actually is.

As I write this forward to Dr. Czinkota's book, the Congress is addressing the complexity of international trade through legislation aimed at increasing American competitiveness in the 21st century. In a just-passed Senate bill, tens of billions of dollars are being allocated to ensure, or so its sponsors claim, that the United States stays at the forefront of technology in semiconductor manufacturing, computer design, telecommunications, biotechnology, and all the other high technology fields that will determine which nation will be the future leader in these fields and which nation will be obliged to follow or to make copies of the technologies that others have pioneered. It was a shock to these Senators to find out that the Chinese company Huawei, which was heavily dependent on research and development carried out in the laboratories that served the Chinese People's Liberation Army, had become the preferred telecommunications equipment for countries around the world that are seeking to install new 5G telecommunications networks. They were competing with our best telecommunications manufacturers and winning.

The House has yet to act. But this situation reminds me of the panic that gripped Congress in the 1950s, when it was realized that the Soviets had launched Sputnik and were ahead of the United States in the space race. It seems that the Congress needs what it perceives to be a hostile challenge to jolt it into action. Today, China provides that incentive to develop a national strategy for technological competitiveness.

Few would doubt that the world is better off with China having lifted more than half a billion people out of poverty and allowed them to reap the beneficiaries of a middle-class life. For their part, even the Chinese Communist leaders would admit that the world trading system that was created in the shadow of the Second World War, with the guidance of United States leadership, played a great role in China's rapid rise. In the 21st century, once China was welcomed as a full partner in the World Trade Organization ("WTO"), and once it promised to adhere to norms of international trade embodied in the WTO, it began to enjoy all the benefits of a full-fledged member of the international trading system. Nevertheless, to say that the WTO was a great benefit to China and that this in turn provided for the basis of world peace and prosperity is not to say that the system is perfect or that it cannot be improved.

The WTO's ability to resolve trade disputes and to set the standards for trade has been recognized by its members to be significantly in need of improvement. The so-called Doha Round, the most recent negotiations organized to achieve those improvements, fell into disarray as the world's great trading nations proved unable to resolve their differences over such issues as dispute resolution, intellectual property, investment, agriculture, and a number of other vexing disagreements. The question of whether there is presently a fair and equitable forum for trade dispute resolution has gotten so bad that the United States Government is currently unwilling to allow a quorum to be established at the WTO's dispute resolution panel. Many other critical issues remain to be resolved before we can say that the WTO is functioning smoothly.

All is not lost. Trade disputes continue to be resolved outside the WTO auspices. Bilateral and multilateral trade agreements with their own separate dispute resolution mechanisms continue to be signed between and among the various regions of the world. In fact, regional trade agreements have supplanted—and in many cases replaced—the WTO as forums for dispute resolution and standard setting. These developments are the context that demonstrates the need for us to understand the dynamics of international trade, all the more.

Michael Czinkota accomplishes what he sets out to do in this book. He brings order and understanding to a chaotic international trading world. The book illustrates what effective marketing can do in the current world trade environment, given the constraints of the trading system. It should be required reading for all serious students of international trade.

—By Dr. Paul Freedenberg

A New Perspective

Professors typically provide a long-term perspective of issues, campaigns, and phenomena. Addressing unprecedented times with historic embeddedness is the key purpose of this book. The past can teach us, not only by understanding what was done before us but also by appreciating the context of changes. The commentary format eliminates the major study approach. Long-term involvement with policy makers and firms has taught me that many people do not read academic books or even high-quality journal articles. Working one's way through them is typically considered too laborious and insufficiently stimulating. However, decision makers do read short pieces, articles, and commentaries. Brevity brings attention but the quality needs to be there. Short writings bring issues to the forefront and capture attention.

Over the decades, international business and trade have mushroomed in importance. Social and economic shifts have taken us from the smoke-filled back-room discussions of experts to public disputes around the world. From ignorance, we may have entered the stage of too much information. A new sense of transparency and accountability offers new directions to businesses and their executives. The emergence of a public moral sense and scrutiny about injustices in connection with many international issues encourages companies and governments to reduce corruption and abandon unsavory practices.

The role of government has changed drastically, first shrinking in the 1980s and 1990s, but now coming back with a vengeance, dictating the direction and strength of international business activities. After decades of aiming for more open markets, even the liberal trading nations and the trade-supporting politicians within them are developing a tendency to restrict imports and encourage exports. In blatant disregard that someone's export has to be someone else's import, governments try to keep home industries protected and their own economies stable and revitalized. Yet, global imbalances are persistent and distortive. We can distinguish patterns of ebb and flow in the international business and trade arena.

Today, we often find the claim that "if it's not on Google it doesn't exist." However, long-term observers recognize that, just like Saint Augustine, who prayed "Lord, make me chaste, but not yet," policy makers and executives often develop strong and nontransparent measures to delay or even defeat the easing of international trade and investment flows. There are also the times where change cannot happen quickly enough, where everyone aims to streamline and fast track legislation.

There are subtle and sometimes not-so-subtle efforts at sanctions and disruptions of trade flows. They are often met by opposing interest levels, which are often from historical developments. When one side loses contracts, blame falls on the corruption and nepotism on part of the winners. Yet, culture may be seen as an obligation to provide for family.

One discusses and often evaluates the meaning and adjustment of key business pillars such as risk, competition, profit, and ownership, which perhaps gradually prepares us for a new environment. Many of today's business executives discover that their activities are but one integral component of society. Politics, security, and religion are only some of the other dimensions that historically, and maybe again in the future, are held in possibly higher esteem than economics and business by society at large. Those who argue based on business principles alone may increasingly find themselves on the losing side.

Each chapter in this book contains opportunities to chew on pressing issues. I hope that the opportunity for comparisons, the recognition of the presence both of rapid shifts and also of permanence, and the appreciation that in many instances the future was 2,000 years ago, provides for good stimuli. Be it for bedtime reading, for beefing up on a topic before a "wise table dinner," or just for racking the brain, I wish you well with these pages.

Washington, DC

CHAPTER 1

International Connectedness

- "The International Dream"

As the largest importer in the world, the United States obtains about 13 percent of global goods and services from other countries—diverse as China, Canada, and Mexico. The United States tends to buy more than it sells. Americans have access to worldwide products and none has to go overseas to get it. But does this mean they have access to everything? And if not, what new inventions and innovations is the United States missing out on?

While everyone talks about exports, we focus on the so often maligned imports. Exports make imports possible, which enhances selection, competition, and competitiveness. With already a shining city on the hill, how can things get even better?

Our team of hands-on experts were exposed to products from around the globe. They are a group of seniors at the McDonough School of Business at Georgetown University. We asked them to give us a closer look into what the United States should import more of. Students explore new motivations for U.S. imports to include goods and services from a wide array of industries ranging from fine foods to health and technology.

Technology has effectively become the center of our lives. Students believe that the United States should dedicate its import efforts on innovative products that will enhance tech performance and connectivity. The United States currently can only support 4G services to telephones. Korea, on the other hand, has been using 5G recently, which has provided them the opportunity to grow faster and be more flexible than the United States. There now is a lucrative market for portable chargers. As they are cheaper to import than to produce, the United States is more likely better off importing battery pack rentals from China.

The need for tech innovation is not limited to mobile phones, but includes automobiles and health. With rising auto tariffs, the United States will have decreasing access to advanced automotive engineering technologies. Specifically, foreign markets sell sleek pickup trucks, which are not available in the United States and penetrate Asia and Sub-Saharan Africa. Access to such advanced forms of auto engineering will benefit U.S. consumers.

Innovation will also support health sector advances. There was demand for robotic goods. Japan was credited with very advanced medical robotics. The Kibo Experiment Module allowed fixing problems on the International Space Station without having to send a human into space. Similarly, robots are used in Japan right now in order to have a more precise and efficient way of significantly treating cancer patients. There are also bionic arms for upper-limb amputees, customizable for each wearer. Children can update their arms as their bodies grow. Such technologies should be brought to the United States, where many individuals have received damage to their limbs.

There also is demand for simple technologies and ideas that effectively improve the wellness and well-being of individuals. Asian face-masks mitigate pollution-related health risks. The Water-Leech—a tank that absorbs and retains water runoff from a shower, bath or sink—was found to be a product worth importing from Australia. This tank allows consumers to save water instead of wasting it down the drain.

Other ideas included public spaces where communities can be given the chance to exercise and socialize in order to become more active and engage with others. Colombia's Ciclovia, where some of the main roads in Bogota are closed off for cars and open to pedestrians who want to bike, walk, or simply chill, inspired such leisure spaces well worth importing.

Discussed was leisure time at work: 2–3 hours for a mid-day nap, otherwise known as siestas. The Spanish's rendition of the traditional American lunch break could potentially attract more millennials into the workplace, and add massive value for employees, particularly those who work in innovative, creative industries.

Cultural innovation was not limited to the workplace. In this increasingly globalized world, it was important to understand different cultures. How do different backgrounds and upbringings result in contrasting approaches to the same situation? Students observed a need for educational exchange programs that remove students from their comfort zones in order to truly experience a variety of different cultures. New exchange programs will completely immerse students into the culture. Most relevant is the opportunity to explore underdeveloped and remote areas of the world, which will eventually be part of everyone's underbelly.

While the United States has access to a range of premium goods and services, imports can be crucial in providing the finer things in life. Students called on the need for luxury, fine foods to task Americans' taste buds. There was strong appeal of wines from France, Italy, and Spain, particularly when paired with refined, imported cheese. Australian marinated goat cheese for $12 per 11oz jar will perhaps be the next luxurious brand of food.

Perceptions of luxury was not limited to goods, but extended also to services. Specifically, in Switzerland, the world-renowned Paracelsus Clinic offers unparalleled medical services that, in a perfect world, would be available in the United States as well. Paracelsus Recovery, founded in

2012, offers a unique "luxury treatment program" for clients struggling with addiction, including substance abuse and mental disorders. Patients live in a luxury residence with a team of international doctors that specialize in their condition. Attention of approximately 15 doctors is solely focused on the patient and their needs. Yet, the cost structure is expensive. At present, the recovery group charges 80,000 Swiss Francs a week, or the equivalent of $81,300.80 USD.

Imports are good, but need to be fair. Our students understand and support such restraints, yet know that selection and diverseness is a strong pivot enriching lives.

- "Let Us Organize World Trade"

There is broad historic agreement that the World Trade Organization (WTO) has been one of the most successful international institutions; its membership accounts for more than 98 percent of world trade. However, today's global economic landscape is changing rapidly, coupled with retrenchment and distancing from multilateral agreements. Combined, these factors impact the discernible value and role of the WTO going forward.

Changed Patterns of Trade and Investment

The expansion and development of IT infrastructure, telecommunications, and computing made the global revolution of the last few decades possible. New technologies, nonexistent when the WTO was established in 1995, have become crucial for growth and development in this decade. The outsourcing revolution has affected the developing world in a major way: global manufacturing and new services have dramatically changed supply chains; corporate espionage and intellectual property infringements supported many corporate changes in developing countries; and WTO negotiations and augmented enforcement procedures have not been able to slow that trend.

Moreover, one of the most critical issues in global trade is the aspect of unprecedented imbalances. Today, China is the new top global merchandise exporter with a total of $2.263 trillion, or 16.25 percent of world exports, according to WTO reports. It is the largest global exporter of goods, 17 percent of world exports, and the third largest importer, 12 percent of global imports.

The United States is the main goods importer with 13.4 percent of the global imports, totaling $2.4 trillion. In 1994, the United States was running an annual merchandise trade deficit of about $120 billion; by 2017, the U.S. annual trade deficit with China alone has ballooned to over $375 billion.

Stalemate at the WTO: Too Big to Be Effective?

The last successful WTO negotiation—the Uruguay Round—was a result of a strengthened, single market in Europe, the creation of the North American Free Trade Agreement (NAFTA), and several plurilateral agreements, such as the Information Technology Agreement (ITA).

The Doha Round of negotiations, beginning in November 2001, aimed to achieve major reforms in the international trading system, with an explicit focus on developing nations. Nevertheless, this premise failed; disagreements concerning the agricultural sector, free trade of services, and intellectual property rights have stalled negotiations.

Twenty years ago, the principal WTO concerns were pollution, global warming, disease, and structural unemployment—none of these agenda items, arguably, have been addressed effectively, much less solved.

Size is also an issue. The WTO is comprised of 164 members, with widely diverse perspectives, levels of development, linkages, and ambitions. The WTO system has become unwieldy because of the unanimity requirement of its voting process. The result: progress with new agreements is at a standstill. Case in point is the reduction of trade tariffs, which, at a global 3 percent of Most Favored Nations status, is at the same level as in 2000.

China: A "Rule Shaker" or a "Rule Maker?"

The West's open invitation for China to join the WTO in 2001 paved the way for its rise to a global economic power. Since then, the balance of power at the WTO has changed dramatically. Chinese outward investment in the global economy has increased thirtyfold, from $7 billion (making up only one percent of the global foreign direct investment (FDI)) to almost $200 billion (13 percent of the global FDI).

China entered the WTO as a "rule taker," evolved into a "rule shaker," and now aims to become a "rule maker."

In fact, economic relations between China, the United States, and the European Union define many of the agreements and disputes at the WTO. Xi Jinping's "China Dream" of national rejuvenation could be seen as a way to reshape the international economic system, putting China at the center.

China has not been an easy partner for the West. Initial optimism that China would turn toward a free market economy has yet to come to fruition. Moreover, with its "capitalism with Chinese characteristics," the country has taken the main benefits of the open trade system by creating major distortions and causing disputes that the WTO lacked the capacity to handle. Controversial issues include intellectual property rights (IPR), free market revisions through government subsidies and state-owned enterprises (SOEs), unequal conditions for market access with major restrictions to market entry in China, and unfair technology transfer. Foreign firms operating in China struggle against restrictive regulations—the government often requires them to hand over their intellectual property as a condition of market access. Asymmetrical market access and lack of reciprocity are magnified further at political levels.

With the existing WTO rule book, it is difficult to hold China accountable. Implications of Chinese "market distortion" and "unfair competitive conditions" consume global trade relations rhetoric; these opinions, voiced loudly by the current U.S. administration, are also shared broadly by other players, such as the European Union and Japan. Owing to high trade deficits, the United States is pushing for WTO reforms, increasing tariffs, and blocking the nominations of seats on the WTO's appellate body (where the United States is a major player in the dispute resolution process) as leverage. Desired reforms aim to regulate market distortions caused by government interventions, simplifying the process of gathering information on unfair trade and investment practices, broadening the scope of banned subsidies, and setting boundaries to proportionate retaliations. But, at the end of the day, why would China agree on reforms that jeopardize its state-run economic model?

The WTO as a Reflection of a "New World"

The WTO does not operate in isolation from changes and new developments impacting trade. In the last two decades, the world's macroeconomic environment was shaken by at least two significant events: the spread of terrorism and the financial crisis of 2008. Terrorism has enhanced the inward focus of the political and economic aspects of national security; the global recession has caused an inward retraction of production and services. International economic issues were largely ignored as attention shifted to domestic job creation, the security and protection of domestic credit markets, and enhancing liquidity. Further, financial and political conflicts seem to foster greater polarization among legislators in many countries around the world.

As a result of continued stalemates and disagreements at the WTO, external actors are adopting a new "do-it-yourself" approach defined by preferential plurilateral trade negotiations—handmade for and benefitting only a limited number of players.

In addition, there is the issue of China's growth in influence. In September 2018, the United States together with the European Union and Japan signed a brief statement voicing shared concerns regarding the future of the WTO, questioning its validity as a primary platform for multilateral trade. As an immediate result of difficult trade relations between the United States and China, and tremendous pressure applied by the current U.S. administration, China afforded European companies access to some sectors, while pledging to co-operate with the European Union on WTO reforms—a decision taken in July 2018 during the EU–China Summit.

Since the appearance of President Xi Jinping at the World Economic Forum two years ago, Beijing has been signaling that it is willing and prepared to assume the role of a new custodian of globalization. However, it seems obvious that China would not accept any reforms at the WTO, or any level, that would jeopardize its own economic model and welfare. At the same time, China wants to preserve the existing global trade order, as the outside world is more crucial than ever for its economic development.

Today's global economic realities are not only introducing a new set of concerns and means of doing business, they are also challenging the very effectiveness of the WTO's historical role as an arbiter of world trade.

- "International Managers Have Choices"

In many areas, politics and law are not immutable. Viewpoints can be modified or even reversed, and new laws can supersede old ones. To achieve change, however, some impetus for it—such as the clamors of a constituency—must occur.

The international manager has various options if rules are disliked.

One high-risk option is to simply ignore prevailing rules and expect to get away with doing so. A second option is to provide input to trade negotiators and expect any problem areas to be resolved in multilateral negotiations. Drawbacks are that this is a time-consuming process, and issues remain outside the control of the firm.

A third option involves the development of coalitions and constituencies that can motivate legislators and politicians to implement change. Even simple changes, such as the way key terms are defined, can positively influence the business environment. Consider, for example, the change in terminology used in the United States to describe trade relations between two nations. For years, attempts to normalize relations with China by granting "most favored nation" (MFN) status drew the ire of objectors who questioned why China deserved to be treated in a "most favored" way. Lost in the debate was the fact that the term "most favored nation" was taken from WTO terminology and indicated only that China would be treated like any other nation for the purpose of trade. When the term was changed to "normal trade relations," tension eased.

Beyond the recasting of definitions, firms can effect change in other ways. A manager may, for example, explain the employment and economic effects of certain laws and regulations and demonstrate the benefits of change. The firm might also enlist the supporting help of local suppliers, customers, and distributors to influence decision makers. The public at large can even be involved through public statements or advertisements calling for action. Developing coalitions is no easy task.

Companies often turn to lobbyists for help, particularly when addressing narrow economic objective or single-issue campaigns. Lobbyists are usually well-connected individuals and firms who can provide access to policy makers and legislators in order to communicate new and pertinent information. Brazilian citrus exporters and computer manufacturers, for example, use U.S. legal and public relations firms to provide them with information about relevant U.S. legislative activity. The Banco do Brasil has used lobbyists to successfully restructure Brazilian debt and establish U.S. banking regulations favorable to Brazil.

Although representation of the firm's interests to government decision makers and legislators is entirely appropriate, the international manager must also consider any potential side effects. Major questions can be raised if such representation becomes very impactful and overt. Short-term gains may be far outweighed by longer-term negative repercussions if the international firm is perceived as bullying or exerting too much political influence.

Based on *Fundamentals of International Business*, 3rd. ed., by Michael R. Czinkota, Ilkka A. Ronkainen, and Michael H. Moffett.

- "The Unspoken Truth about International Business"

Language has been described as the mirror of culture. Language itself is multidimensional. This is true not only of the spoken word but also of the nonverbal language of international business.

Messages are conveyed not just by the words used but also by how those words are spoken and through such nonverbal means as gestures, body position, and eye contact. These nonverbal actions and behaviors reveal hidden clues to culture.

Five key topics—time, space, body language, friendship patterns, and business agreements—offer a starting point from which managers can begin to acquire the understanding necessary to do business in foreign countries.

Understanding national and cultural differences in the concept of time is critical for an international business manager. In many parts of the world, time is flexible and is not seen as a limited commodity; people come late to appointments or may not come at all.

In Mexico for instance, it is not unusual to show up at 1:45 p.m. for a 1:00 p.m. appointment. Although a late afternoon siesta cuts apart the business day, businesspeople will often be at their desks until 10 o'clock at night.

In Hong Kong, too, it is futile to set exact meeting times because getting from one place to another may take minutes or hours, depending on traffic.

Showing indignation or impatience at such behavior would astonish an Arab, Latin American, or Asian.

Perception of time also affects business negotiations. Asians and Europeans tend to be more interested in long-term partnerships, while Americans are eager for deals that will be profitable in the short term, meaning less than a year.

Individuals vary in their preferences for personal space. Arabs and Latin Americans like to stand close to people when they talk. If an American who may not be comfortable at such close range, backs away from an Arab, this might incorrectly be perceived as a negative reaction.

An interesting exercise is to compare and contrast the conversation styles of different nationalities. Northern Europeans are quite reserved in using their hands and maintain a good amount of personal space, whereas Southern Europeans involved their bodies to a far greater degree in making a point.

International body language, too, can befuddle international business relations.

For example, an American manager may after successful completion of negotiations, impulsively give a finger-and-thumb "okay" sign. In southern France, this would signify the deal was worthless, and in Japan, it would mean that a little bribe had been requested. The gesture would be grossly insulting to Brazilians.

Misunderstanding nonverbal cues can undermine international negotiations. While Eastern and Chinese negotiators usually lean back and make frequent eye contact while projecting negativity, Western negotiators usually avert their gaze for the same purpose.

In some countries, extended social acquaintance and the establishment of appropriate personal rapport are essential to conducting business. The feeling is that one should know one's business partner on a personal level before transactions can occur.

Therefore, rushing straight to business will not be rewarded because deals are made on the basis of not only the best product or price but also the entity or person deemed most trustworthy. Contract may be bound on handshakes, not lengthy and complex agreements—a fact that makes some, especially Western, businesspeople uneasy.

Excerpt from *Fundamentals of International Business, 3rd ed.,* by Michael R. Czinkota, Ilkka A. Ronkainen, and Michael H. Moffett

- "Global Medical Tourism"

Medical tourism can be traced to 4000 BC—when Greek pilgrims would sail abroad to seek the healing power of hot springs and baths. Over the past two decades, the industry encountered dramatic shifts.

Once wealthy patients from emerging economies sought treatments not available in their home countries. Since the new millennium, however, the flow of patients goes in the other direction. Rising health care costs prompt travelers from advanced economies to seek international destinations offering lower-cost or timelier alternatives to domestic care.

For instance, a spinal fusion in the United States costs an average of $110,000 in 2016. The same procedure was $6,150 in Vietnam. Heart bypass surgery, which costs $123,000 in the United States in 2016, is $12,100 in Malaysia. For many patients from high-priced countries, the solution is clear—it pays to seek medical care abroad!

The size of such tourism has ballooned since the late 1990s. Its value ranges between US$45.5 billion and $72 billion in 2017, with approximately 14 to 16 million patients seeking medical care beyond their countries' borders.

Modern medical tourism is a global phenomenon. Traditional models emphasized internationalization as an incremental procedure. But the industry surged after the Asian financial crisis of 1997, which drove hospitals in Malaysia, Singapore, and Thailand to seek patients from abroad. They had already undergone substantial modernization, catering to a domestic middle class that demanded medical services commensurate with their newly acquired wealth. With the economic downturn, however, a shrinking middle class could no longer afford these superior facilities. International clients provided a ready solution to an excess supply of private medical facilities.

The success of hospitals in Southeast Asia inspired other countries toward medical tourism. Regional hubs emerged due to advantages of geographical proximity and specialization. Malaysia and Singapore, for instance, received an influx of patients from Indonesia, while many patients in India came from Africa and the Middle East. Brazil, Costa Rica, and Mexico all benefited from their proximity to the United States.

A clear pattern has emerged in the lifecycle of medical industries. First, countries in the developing world begin to offer services similar to those found in advanced economies. As new segments of international health care populations emerge, just like sun flowers, new medical tourism destinations grow toward the new opportunity. Close proximity to wealthy consumers constitute a competitive edge. To retain their market share, leading destinations formulate new strategies and options.

In order to survive growing competition, hospitals in emerging nations tend to implement two strategies. Since technologies stem from post-industrialized countries, most can only imitate. Their novelty comes from specialization in specific medical procedures. Doing few tasks very often improves capability, capacity, and efficiency, and thus improves reputational success.

However, this tactic may be ineffective as other hospitals develop similar capabilities. Consumer preferences will hinge on how closely services comply with their own cultural preferences and norms. Hospitals attract patients based on familiarity with local approaches and usages. Such an approach gives room for the increasingly recognized component of holistic healing.

It is important to understand how the lifecycle of hospitals continues to evolve. Different stakeholders—from governments to accreditation services to health care providers to patients themselves—will be affected by the expansion of the industry. For example, to date, there is still much unfounded reluctance to accept health care services offered by international sources. Once the industry manages to break out of restrictive domestic silos, a fundamental reconfiguration of service and cost will be the consequence. Let's look forward to that!

Nittaya Wongtada is a Professor at the NIDA Business School of the National Institute of Development Administration, in Bangkok, Thailand.

This comment is based on the article "Transformation in the Global Medical Tourism Industry," Transylvania Review, Vol. 25, 2017.

- "A World without international marketing?"

Sometimes we only know what we lost when it has left us. I put this thought to the test in my class of Georgetown University students. In our course "Marketing Across Borders," we worked on the question: "What would life look like without international marketing?" The answers offered various perspectives reflecting their interest and training in international affairs. The range was broad, addressing the impact of international marketing in the context of diversity, choices, cultural exchange, and international quality standards.

On a personal level, students saw substantial impact of international marketing on their lives. Some mentioned that international marketing and its activities creates thousands of jobs around the world. This was seen as highly relevant to themselves, but they included their parents as well since such a change clearly involved today and the future. Some students said that without international marketing a life would be simpler but not necessarily in a good way. International marketing was seen to bring to life a variety of products that enrich consumers and make them more productive.

Some respondents highlighted the exposure to new thoughts and ideas that international marketing brings to people around the world. Such exposure motivates the competition between companies to supply better quality combined with better value. This competition leads to innovation in products across different markets around the world. Without international marketing, the high-quality standards we have today would diminish due to decreasing competition.

Companies would also feel the absence of international marketing. Expansion across borders will be harder and would have to rely without marketing heavily on word-of-mouth communication. Exports and imports will be far less than today's value since international activities will be less profitable. Selling products to other cultures in which they are not interested will be difficult. Companies will have fewer opportunities to learn and develop from others as well. Problems will be caused by a lack of willingness to adjust or a lack of motivation to develop and compete. In consequence, the world won't be as efficient as today.

There was the hypothesis that international marketing is likely to reduce poverty and increase international cooperation. These benefits would disappear when FDI decreases. Sales in foreign markets would diminish without the lubricating effect of international marketing. Less cultural awareness of others would be the consequence of a decline in intercultural communication. Companies would be less socially responsible and transparent as they won't be inspired by other international companies that serve international communities. This would newly insert more psychic distance between cultures and countries, and reduce the attention paid to common problems and actions taken for the public good.

Finally, we explored what students would miss most, where does the pain threshold begin: We know about the wide variety of products that are moved and brought to market, thanks to marketing. So how about the loss of video games, cars, music tourism, or even commercials. These items were touched on, but the core of items one would miss the most was Food, Food, and Food again. Students were quite varied in their thinking as long as the items whose loss was deplored dealt with sustenance or alimentation. Leading among products held dear were chocolate, snacks, noodles, candies, and anything else which could be eaten by chopstick. Quite a broad base from students whose parents were only introduced to new eating utensils. Food and its variety tend to give staying power to globalization and also encourage cross fertilization. Let it give new opportunity to a life with spice.

- "Offsets: One answer to International Trade Imbalances"

When foreign governments shop for defense supplies, they are not solely motivated by price and quality. In light of the trade balance effects of major acquisitions such as aircraft or defense products, international customers often require U.S. vendors to purchase goods from them in order to "offset" the trade balance effects large purchases have on their trade flows. In light of enormous U.S. trade deficits, it is time for the United States to reciprocate with offset demands of our trading partners. Frequently, we find ourselves in conditions where foreign sales to us are major and our sales to importers and their nations are minor. This leads to trade relations that are out of kilter. U.S. firms have accommodated foreign offset demands for decades. Now is the time when some give-back by our trading partners is the right medicine to improve world trade imbalances.

Offsets are industrial compensation arrangements demanded (so far only) by foreign governments as a condition for making major purchases, such as military hardware. Sometimes, these arrangements are directly related to the goods being traded. For instance, the Spanish air force's planes—American-made McDonnell Douglas F/A-18 Hornets— use rudders, fuselage components, and speed brakes made by Spanish companies. U.S. sellers of the planes have provided the relevant technology information so that Spanish firms are now successful new producers in the industry. Under offset conditions, U.S. companies also often help export a client country's goods go international, or even support the performance of tourism services. For example, the "Cleopatra Scheme" allowed foreign suppliers to Egypt to meet their agreed-upon offset obligations through package tours for international tourists.

In 2015, U.S. firms entered into 38 new offset agreements where they agreed to cause purchases with 15 countries valued at $3.1 billion. In 2017, the total U.S. trade deficit was $566 billion after it imported $2.895 trillion of goods and services while exporting $2.329 trillion. No country has a bigger trade surplus with the United States than China. In 2017, the U.S. deficit with China climbed to its highest level on record, amounting to a gap of $375 billion.

Eliminating imbalances is a core component of the Trump administration's international economic policy. One policy approach has been the threat of tariffs against China. One effective supplemental strategy could be the instigation of offset agreements with major trade surplus nations.

For instance, many American imports that contribute to the trade deficit are capital goods, such as computers and telecom equipment. An offset agreement between China and the United States could require China to use American-made components, perhaps even from Chinese-owned plants. An example could be the export of Smithfield ham from the United States to be served in company cafeterias in China. Then there are excellent opportunities for Chinese tourists, particularly if equipped with high-spend budgets.

The American trade deficit is not easily resolved. Government would be well served to explore nontraditional options in order to develop more than one fulcrum for leverage. New use of offset agreements—which have provided our trading partners with past success at our expense—could help revitalize American industries and bring a new sense of balance to trade relationships. Our government should encourage offset commitments by foreign firms and countries who sell a lot to us. America deserves to reap the benefits!

• "The Secret to Trade Policy Success"

University teaching is again in session. As in past summer and fall semesters, I teach international business at both Georgetown University in Washington, DC and at Kent University in Canterbury, UK.

With students I note three different categories of sentiments, quite telling of voting tendencies. Two virtually equal blocs boast firmly established perspectives with little room for flexibility. Between them are the persons most crucial for policy and politics: hedonists. They seek to enjoy life, adopt views of happiness and comfort, and, in all likelihood, determine the key prize: election victory!

At Kent, discussions will oftentimes center around the political disputes surrounding the British exit from the European Union and the outcomes of new steps taken by Prime Minister Boris Johnson.

Students and faculty are highly aware that the value of the pound is declining against the dollar and that some beach houses near Kent are for sale. However, this is only relevant to those who need dollars or want to sell a beach house. Some seem to value education less, which leads to a drop in student enrollment and translates into less public support for universities. Overall, dislocations are mainly seen as temporary phenomena—so no major changes by voters and businesses are implemented or expected. Even if there are shifts, primary attention rests with the British Isles, not with the rest of the world.

At Georgetown, there is great interest in international business as illustrated in my seminar on "International Trade: 'The Insiders'." Students were given the following prompt, "In case of a trade war, which international products would you be willing to give up and which ones would you stress to keep?"

Students generally agreed they could not do without their foreign-made consumer electronics and technology. "I am extremely reliant on Chinese made Apple products in my everyday life," was a typical statement.

Low-tech was important too. Examples were an unwillingness to sacrifice foreign pencils and pens, because of other countries' comparative advantage in quality and price.

There was a split and much disagreement regarding clothing. Some believed it would be a necessary industry to bring back to the United States. Others felt the increase in prices would hurt low-income and middle-class families, an issue of personal responsibility or promulgated by those who enjoy the good life.

Respondents also disagreed on automobiles. Some felt U.S. consumers should have access to foreign automobiles, because they "tend to be of higher quality in luxury, performance, and fuel economy." Those who believe that the United States should stop importing cars also extol the value of public transportation and environmentally friendly options. Economic resurgence of domestic manufacturers was seen as a side benefit. Stop importing products known for exploiting child labor or using harmful labor practices was a strong sentiment.

Food issues drew mixed opinions. Some felt that the United States should feed its residents with domestically produced goods only, while others believed that autarky with domestic agriculture would erode quality of life and hurt the environment. Values were important. Tobacco and other socially harmful products should be abandoned.

Proponents for giving up foreign steel cited America's heart-warming history. With its production, the United States used to have a steel industry that was respected, widespread, moderately effective, and an important employer.

Personal experiences influence what one is willing to give up. "I would sacrifice olives from Greece because I have them right now and I don't eat them," said one. "I have a surplus of nylon clothing that is definitely [not] necessary considering how little I actually go to the gym," admitted another. "I don't want to sacrifice my eating preferences under any circumstances," a Nutella lover wrote.

Differences in reasoning by students who are the upcoming "young tigers" reflect diverse perspectives, priorities, and preferences. There was little room or willingness to change one's views. Consequently, any new trade policy will require room for implementation and will face strong variance of support.

Americans have large and acceptable self-interest, which must be understood by policy makers. I perceive personal self-oriented desires to account for approximately one-fourth of the tipping power leading to decisions. These special needs and expectations must be recognized, affirmed, appealed to, and rewarded with clear commitments to make and fulfill promises. Ignoring the smiles, the pleasures, and the extent to which life is affected by policy and its collateral effects is done at one's own peril. It's not all economics!

- "Socialism Slows Progress"

My annual assessment of the intellectual and economic proximity between both the United States and Europe indicates ongoing disenchantment and a growing psychic distance from each other. Conditions have changed not all for the better, perhaps because of the thriving growth of socialist thinking. The public preference given to the group over the individual is dangerous to the quality of life in both regions.

England used to stand out for the views and perspectives by its educated experts on money and markets. Now they don't know and don't care. New announcements and shifts are just shrugged off or, worse yet, ignored. Refusing to think or getting involved is the equivalent of Socrates' poisoned hemlock cup—because conditions will not improve by themselves.

British institutions, which label themselves as European, need to rethink their position as to its meaning in times of Brexit. Prime Minister Johnson may not defuse conflicts and polarization. How to help ship captains make a choice between the drowning migrants and personal jail time for their rescue? Are we all in the same boat? Even in theater performances the audience and troupe performances have lost their traditional bite.

Germany has a whole set of growing problems. I am not referring to the physical tremors of Chancellor Merkel. When standing is a problem she can sit. In the United States, President Roosevelt served the country despite difficult illnesses, for more than three terms.

But I am concerned about the diminution of German ability to rely on its traditional strengths. When German intellectuals talk about U.S. policies there is very little well-formed reasoning, or even desire for input and learning. Rather, flash judgments and condemnations are made, remindful of the checking of boxes.

When the official airplanes of both the chancellor and the president repeatedly either can't fly or must return to land right after take-off, then the motto of "advancement through technology" does not fare very well. Misleading public information on air contamination by car diesel engines is a shameful event. Failed technology to measure societal impact of government action is wasteful and inefficient. Expropriation of rental property owners will do little to increase the housing stock.

Increasingly, a sense of proportion and morality is missing. Take the case of Gustl Mollath who was wrongfully placed in a psychiatric ward for more than seven years, after complaining about banking irregularities. Now, the government offers him a paltry compensation of less than $200,000. At the same time, the Deutsche Bank provides publicly more than $10 million for ineffective managers to depart, and we don't yet know about any additional hidden support.

The Nordic countries have lots of goods available but few of them are thrilling. The food offered, for example, was surely healthy, but not appetizing. Drinks were hard to get, even at events where conviviality was the objective, not a by-product. Big praise to the person who found and handed in my disappeared wallet. Thank you, Gary, from the West Coast!

European country governments regulate many things, issues, and interactions, a form of localized socialism I suppose. But it means fewer and quite expensive taxis, no Ubers, little adjustment to changing conditions. New government thinking stresses more taxes.

France, for example, tries to impose a new 3 percent tax on large digital companies.

Italy still has very good wines and beautiful bridges from Roman days, but roads are decaying, and modern bridges are crumbling. Speed and parsimony cannot be the only criterion for quality public projects. Modes of transport appear to be routinely under strike during times of heavy use. Austrian government leaders are caught on tape offering the wholesale transfer of government contracts.

People seem content, but not driven or forward oriented. Many tasks are either left unfulfilled or waiting for foreign hands, which both the public and the private sector appear to encourage.

Overarching governing by the European Union seems to be often haphazard, contradicting the desires of the citizens affected. Leadership selection often brings on candidates who govern in spite, not because of themselves. Will the new team of Ursula von der Leyen make its mark with a reduction of regulation? All in all, it's great to be exposed to history, and remember the British Pound as world currency, Greek and Roma palazzi, Marie Antoinette's cakes, and the Viking battles. But for now, innovation, change, and a forward-looking perspective give good future odds to America.

- "Action and Imagery in the Middle East May Be Worth It"

President Donald Trump ordered the termination of Major General Qassim Soleimani of Iran in retribution for his terrorist plans and activities. Iran retaliated with a missile strike on Iraqi bases hosting U.S. troops. As the result, the president announced new economic sanctions against Tehran. Many now wonder whether this United States's involvement is worth it.

But these exchanges are mostly imagery. Our policy planners need to have a vision of how our relationship with the world should be 20 years from now. Future generations should know that our policies, activities, efforts, and investments were worth the effort.

At issue is the long-term outcome of these policy measures. Today, if you ask the State Department for travel advice, you will be referred to the "Travel Warnings" website. On it, you will find many admonitions of where not to go and what not to do. For example, the State Department issued a global security alert on January 8, 2020, to warn U.S. citizens of heightened tension in the Middle East. Americans are advised to "keep a low profile, avoid demonstrations or large gatherings, be aware of surroundings and stay alert in locations frequented by tourists."

The travel advisory puts Iran on a Level 4: Do Not Travel, which indicates growing risk of kidnapping, arrest, and detention of U.S. citizens. Iraq and Syria are also ranked Level 4 due to terrorism, kidnapping, and armed conflict. U.S. citizens who decide to travel to Iraq or Syria are advised to "draft a will and designate appropriate insurance beneficiaries and/or power of attorney" and to "discuss a plan with loved ones regarding care/custody of children, pets, funeral wishes, etc."

All these measures are helpful, but what is needed is continued long-term thinking as to how we will achieve globally a rating of Level 1 as we have for Canada and Hungary, which encourages travel with normal precautions. Being American should eventually be a sign of safety and security, as it was for the biblical St. Paul. A brief review of the life of St. Paul, also called the 13th apostle, may provide guidance and inspiration. His birth name was Saul. He was a Jew and converted to Christianity. He was born in Tarsus of the Roman Empire, which made him a Roman citizen. He was an indefatigable traveler, an early globalist who wrote lots of letters, many of which significantly challenged the status quo, and therefore were written missives equivalent to many missiles. He established churches in Asia Minor. He evangelized in Macedonia, Thessalonica, Athens, Corinth, and Malta. During his life and travels, he was often met with great hostility and persecution. The Roman emperor himself was none too pleased with Paul's preaching and traveling. In an era of multideities, Christianity was not exactly popular in the reigning circles of the day.

What are the lessons here? St. Paul reached out to the world. His message was controversial, but it has survived quite well until today. He was not popular for his message—but he got the word out. He did not hesitate to go to the far corners of the world of his day. In spite of all the controversy and hatred that he faced, the people he encountered abroad did not harm him. Even when he was a captive in the provinces, he was untouchable and treated with respect and hospitality because he was protected by his citizenship of Rome.

St. Paul's circumstances can be our guide for a vision of the future. We are proud to be Americans and the world should know it. There are special conditions associated with American citizenship—and our exposure and policies should enhance rather than hide that fact.

Some of that "specialness" is reflected in our international policies. In a statement addressing the nation the day after the strike against Major General Soleimani, President Trump stated that "under my leadership, America's policy is unambiguous to terrorists who harm or intend to harm any American. We will find you. We will eliminate you. We will always protect our diplomats, service members, all Americans, and our allies."

In order to find out whether the effort was worth it, we should see where we are in the next generation. By then, when requesting a travel advisory from the State Department, here is what I'd like to see: "As a traveler, you are advised to carry identification of being a U.S. citizen with you at all times. Wear an American flag pin to let everyone know that you are an American. This way, you will carry an umbrella of respect, safety and security. Remember, you represent your country. We wish you success in your travels."

Some might think of such a vision as perhaps lacking in humility. I see it as a worthwhile goal to strive for, as a translation of a national effort onto individual well-being, and as an outcome that will truly help bring peace to the world. After all, if Americans are secure, others will be as well.

A National Export Assistance Policy for New and Growing Businesses

Exporting is one of many market expansion activities of the firm. As such, exporting is similar to looking for new customers in the next town, the next state, or on the other coast; it differs only in that national borders are crossed, and international accounts and currencies are involved. Yet, these differences make exports special from a policy perspective. From a macro perspective, exports are special because they can affect currency values and the fiscal and monetary policies of governments, shape public perception of competitiveness, and determine the level of imports a country can afford. Abroad, exports augment the availability and choice of goods and services for individuals, and improve the standard of living and quality of life. On the level of the firm, exports offer the opportunity for economies of scale. By broadening its market reach and serving customers abroad, a firm can produce more and do so more efficiently, which is particularly important if domestic sales are below breakeven levels. As a result, the firm may achieve lower costs and higher profits both at home and abroad. Through exporting the firm benefits from market diversification, taking advantage of different growth rates in different markets, and gaining stability by not being overly dependent on any particular market. Exporting also lets the firm learn from the competition, makes it sensitive to different demand structures and cultural dimensions, and proves its ability to survive in a less familiar environment in spite of higher transaction costs. All these lessons can make the firm a stronger competitor at home. Finally, since exporting is only one possible international marketing strategy, it may well lead to the employment of additional strategies such as direct foreign investment, joint ventures, franchising, or licensing—all of which contribute to the growth and economic strength of the firm, and, on an aggregate level, to the economic security of a nation.

Many see the global market as the exclusive realm of large, multinational corporations. It is commonly explained that almost half of U.S. exports are made by the 100 largest corporations, and that 80 percent of U.S. exports are carried out by only 2,500 firms. Overlooked is the fact that thousands of smaller sized firms have been fueling an U.S. export boom, which has supported the economy in times of limited domestic growth. A large portion of export shipments from the United States are for less than $10,000 and there are more than 100,000 U.S. firms that export at least occasionally. The reason for this export success of smaller firms lies in the new determinants of competitiveness, as framed by the wishes and needs of the foreign buyers. Other than in the distant past, where price alone was at the forefront, buyers today also expect an excellent product fit, high levels of corporate responsiveness, a substantial service orientation, and high corporate commitment. New and growing firms stack up well on all these dimensions compared to their larger brethren, and may even have a competitive advantage. Take the issue of product fit. In today's era of niche marketing, where specialization rather than mass production is prized, the customization of operations is often crucial. In a large corporate system, changes are often subject to delays as various layers of management are consulted, costs recalculated, and multiple communication levels exercised. In a smaller operation, procedures can more easily be adopted to the special needs of the customer or to local requirements. Smaller firms can offer clearer lines of accountability since the decision maker can be more visible and responsive to the customer. During negotiations, or later on, if something does not go according to plan, the customer knows whom to contact to fix the problem. Smaller firms are better equipped to handle exceptions. Since international sales situations have high variability, either in terms of the timing or the nature of the sale, a smaller firm can provide a more flexible framework for the decision process. Exceptions can be handled when they occur rather than after waiting for concurrence from other levels of the organization. Smaller firms offer their customers better inward and outward communication linkages, which are direct between the provider of a service or product and its user. The result is a short response time. If a special situation should arise, response can be immediate, direct, and predictable to the customer, providing precisely those competitive ingredients that reduce risk and costs.

Smaller firms also have the most to gain from the experience curve effects of exporting. Research by the Boston Consulting Group has shown that each time cumulative output of a firm doubles, the costs on value added decrease between 20 and 30 percent. Owing to the small original base, it is much easier for a new or growing business to double cumulative output and reap the resulting benefits than it is for a large established firm. Most importantly, once a small firm goes international, it usually does so with the full commitment of the owner and top management. The foreign customer therefore knows that this is an activity, which has the management's heart and soul behind it. In today's times where we are moving, on a global level, away from transaction marketing and toward relationship marketing, such a perception is crucial in providing the winning edge.

CHAPTER 2

Cultures in Play

- "Spargelzeit"

In Germany, there is now an important season highlighting the special value of white asparagus. Anyone who visits Germany between April and June will certainly remember a truly national food specialty: white asparagus together with melted butter and ham.

German food culture is quite precise when it comes to timing. The Spargel season has been long established as a seasonal spring product from April to June. This is the framework outside of which it is considered inappropriate to consume white asparagus. One famous example is the consumption of white sausage (Weißwurst) in Bavaria. Whether eaten at home or in a restaurant, a consumer of this sausage will be looked down upon for eating it once the noon Church bell has rung.

One important deadline issue often surrounds the harvesting of asparagus. In the 2020 asparagus season, the white gold must be harvested, distributed, and consumed. All prepare for the season, but circumstances like health care problems can severely disrupt the harvest. The product was there, but the harvesters were not. To outrace the time of product availability, many efforts were undertaken. Since the season ends on June 24, and all consumers and producers say goodbye to their favorite stalks, it is crucial to do the digging when the timing is good. This time around, the federal government was implored by asparagus farmers to help with the harvest. A major effort was made to attract volunteers among students and teachers to dig up the asparagus (which is why the vegetable is white rather than green). Alas, no success. In spite of good pay and substantial enthusiasm for agricultural processes, many of the "volunteers" did not return on day two of the exercise. The strain on the lower back was just too great. I sensed a major culinary conflict coming about: would good Germans miss out on one of their favorite foods just because academics were incapable servants of agriculture? What would come next in the cultural loss—perhaps the abandonment of the Leberknödelsuppe (liver dumpling soup)? Or might it even be the sacrosanct Schweinshaxe (pork shank with Kraut)? For a time, German (particularly Bavarian) culinary choice was downtrodden. But the cuisine of asparagi was saved by the bell.

In spite of overarching migration, of which one might have expected limits to the inflow of agricultural workers, a solution was found; 40,000 special work visas were issued for Polish workers. It is simply too risky to leave asparagus harvesting to the asparagus growers. We know the task must be completed. Politically, the issue is a crucial one because asparagus appears to contribute remarkably to German contentment. Let us not run afoul of national expectations, particularly since in Poland itself, domestic harvesters were standing ready and able to distribute the goods. Bureaucratic flexibility brought on the visitor visas. This year's harvest of asparagus is again secure. If a country needs a helping hand, it can often be found outstretched in the international market.

Polish workers are encouraged to use their forte while critical for the agricultural impact. Already at this time, new technologies like those produced in California and Hungary may very well take over for harvesting by hand. But then, German asparagus may be too sacred to be conducted by machines. Time will tell.

- "Commonality Builds a Bridge"

International business complexity calls for commonality. The need for and acceptance of the soul builds up a common path and provides a joint perspective underpinned by a broadly supported objective.

Rising global communication and output from a global labor force have created a growing and diverse marketplace. Changes include the contrast and juncture of controversial debates over international trade, artificial intelligence, refugees, terrorism, and greatly intensify the complexity of international business.

Commonality is increasingly difficult, yet important to achieve for the sake of relationship and trust building in international business. The understanding of the soul and its accompanying emotional subcomponents provides individuals, companies, and countries with the opportunity to develop and align global values and bridges between them. If people act and argue focused on business principles alone, they may find themselves increasingly ignored.

New thinking and behavior regarding collaboration are needed to help employees work across cultures. According to the World Bank, the global labor force has reached almost 3.5 billion in 2018. A shortage of skilled workers may intensify competition for talent.

Owing to a lack of local knowledge, unfamiliarity with market conditions, insufficient insights into consumer behavior, and newness to political decision making, foreign firms typically face shortcomings and disadvantages when entering a new market. The overarching umbrella is provided by the soul, which affects judgment and offers simplicity. It allows the understanding of truth and enables good decision making in light of changing realities. For example, negotiators who lose tend to blame their loss on the corruption and nepotism of winners. Yet, culturally, the closeness to family and desire to help one's own environment can be seen as a supportive obligation rather than a deviation. How good it is to lay off blame and recognize the conditionality of behavior and management.

The soul and its key pillars such as politics, security, and religion can teach new entrants more and prepare them better than mere principles of economics and business.

Some lessons can be taken from history, which permeates our lives but is usually forgotten. We bemoan the disruptions from terrorism but neglect that the Crusaders already wrote home about their fear of terror. We debate new approaches of artificial intelligence in teaching and communication, but don't recall the effects that Gutenberg's printing press of 1440, wireless telegraphy, or the introduction of radio had on business and society. We deplore the differentiation of groups based on religion but conveniently forget the impact of Torquemada, the Inquisition, or the reactions to Luther's theses on the church doors of Wittenberg.

Retrospection of the far-reaching consequences of past international conflicts and reconciliations may bring some new insights to the solution of complexity. Not all measures are equal at all times. Tariffs, for example, can be a tool to deal with crises and promote trade.

International marketing offers a new linkage in cultures and values. New progress in thinking and behavior can and must shape a greater global commonality in values.

- "Fish and Chips, All the Time?"

Applicants for British citizenship face a rigorous test with some questions too obscure even for natives. According to a mock test for its British staff, the *Wall Street Journal* found that many couldn't answer the questions correctly.

The compulsory citizenship test was first announced in 2002. Lord David Blunkett, home secretary at the time, initiated the test. Originally, it aimed to help people know things that make local life easy and safe. Tony Blair's government also wanted to show encouragement and welcome immigrants via the test. Now, the test is up for review. What does it mean to be British? Here are some examples.

Where did the people of the Bronze Age bury their dead? Who first introduced "shampooing" to the United Kingdom? Does "having the ability to laugh at oneself" represent an important part of the British character? Do the British eat fish and chips for every lunch?

Immigrants must pass such mandatory questions in order to obtain British citizenship. The test has become harder in reaction to the surge of aspiring Britons from emerging nations. Given Brexit and Britain's possible drop-out from the European Union, more Europeans are also taking the test to ensure their right to remain in the United Kingdom.

By comparison, Switzerland also has a naturalization test based on acculturation. The State Secretariat for Migration examines whether applicants are integrated in the Swiss way of life, familiar and accepting of Swiss customs and traditions, able to comply with the Swiss rule of law, and not threatening Switzerland's internal or external security.

The Swiss government also makes its naturalization test harder as of 2018. Swiss migration regulations seem stricter than the United Kingdom's. A non-EU citizen can apply for a Swiss permanent residence permit after living in Switzerland for 10 years. Naturalization as a Swiss citizen takes 12 years, while in the United Kingdom it takes only 5 years. Passing the test is only the start of a process rather than a guarantee of citizenship.

The oral test for language assessment seems to be a particular obstacle for many applicants. But yodeling is not required. "What would you say is typically Swiss?"is a question on the Swiss citizenship test. Swiss women with a gold lace cap preparing the Cheese Fondue for her family might be the first image to pop out your head. But is that always true?

It's interesting that when you search the term "British citizenship test" or "Swiss citizenship test" on Google, the first page results will mainly offer test preparation services. The cottage industry coaching applicants for the citizenship test has become increasingly popular. Owing to harder tests and stricter application processes, this industry will likely expand substantially in the near future.

Is it time to rethink the concept of a citizenship test? Should there be only one version of a country's culture? How can governments identify different characteristics of citizens and translate those into behavioral norms, especially in the diverse European environment? Diversity makes life not only more interesting but also more unexpected. There is much enjoyment nowadays with many different foods, fashions, and habits in the United Kingdom and Switzerland. What is the value and price of homogeneity?

There might well be a need to insist on a common spirituality supporting national underpinnings. Some criteria may need to be adjusted and individual support of them affirmed for citizenship to work! Otherwise people are visitors, a fine and useful role, but different from citizens. Not everyone needs fish and chips for lunch. How about dumplings? Or hot dry noodles?

- "In the Interest of Food"

While around the globe we all celebrate some form of Thanksgiving, the food consumed does vary. In the United States we consume turkey— usually store bought, not hunted. Bavaria sees such celebration with beer and bratwurst. In China, the celebratory meal consists of tea and hotpot.

"Everything can be solved by a hotpot. If not, it can be solved by two." These words are popular in China. A staple comfort food, the hotpot is a symbol of Chinese leisure life and culture. Similar to the French cheese fondue, the traditional Chinese dish consists of a communal pot in which small ingredients are dipped. The ritual always involves gathering around the dining table, with a large hot pot of broth placed at the center. While simmering, the broth is then enriched by fresh and raw ingredients. These include finely cut meats, vegetables, tofu, and seafood that are cooked in the broth.

The dish can be found in homes and in restaurants across China and other parts of Asia. Recently, the hotpot found its way in other regions around the world as HaiDiLao International Holding Ltd.— China's largest hotpot restaurant group in terms of sales—gained market shares abroad. Most hotpot restaurants will attempt to distinguish themselves with their unique flavors and taste, but nothing compares to HaiDiLao's secret recipe.

Aside from the delicious hotpot, HaiDiLao's success is due to its remarkable service strategy. HaiDiLao aspires to make every customer feel special. Outside the restaurants, customers line up at the door, waiting with great patience as they indulge in HaiDiLao's complimentary services. Such services range from free snacks and beverages to free massages and manicures. Once customers enter the restaurant, waiters greet them, always with a smile, while subsequently taking their order with speed and accuracy. If dining alone, the restaurant provides its customers with a stuffed toy to be seated in front of them, in order to keep them company.

Although the hotpot restaurant business is extremely competitive, the chain succeeded in standing out from other hotpot restaurants by creating the ultimate dining experience. Branches are managed directly by a shared and central distribution network, ensuring the standardization of food quality across all its stores. By offering exceptional customer service, and adopting a supply chain management system, all HaiDiLao subsidiaries tend to fulfill, and at times exceed, customer expectations.

Gaining increasing popularity in China, plans call for the chain to enter overseas markets, including the United Kingdom and Canada. In late September, HaiDiLao presented an IPO to help fund and continue its expansion. Initially priced at $2.27 per share, the public offering gave the firm a valuation of about $12 billion. Some people may argue that HaiDiLao's IPO value is a bit high, considering its lack of success in the United States.

Back in 2013, HaiDiLao opened its first U.S. restaurant in Arcadia, California. The restaurant received negative reviews on Yelp and less and less customer retention. Reviewers complained about HaiDiLao's overpriced menu, and intrusive and incompetent staff service. Despite its roaring success in China, the company failed to stand out in the United States and was proven to be a big disappointment.

Fast forward to today—with an international expansion right around the corner, how can HaiDiLao succeed outside of China? HaiDiLao will have to face more than its competing hotpot counterparts and learn from its mistakes with the earlier U.S. expansion. Challenges will also come from the local food industry, including other comfort foods such as hamburgers and hot dogs.

In overseas markets, new conditions will apply. First, the chain needs to develop a differentiation strategy by offering complimentary services that are less intrusive and that adhere to U.S. standards. Since offering mani-pedis would be considered a health code violation and waiting to hand tissue paper to customers after washing their hands would seem strange, HaiDiLao needs to tailor its services to fit the American market's wants and needs. Such services comprise complimentary hair ties, phone chargers, restroom grooming kits, and an iPad ordering system. They also provide video conferencing rooms, in which customers can enjoy their hotpot experience while video chatting.

Additionally, the firm needs to focus on the product and pricing strategy. Chinese food in the United States is still labeled as inexpensive, fast food. HaiDiLao prices its authentic dining experience between $30 and $50 per person, which may seem costly to American customers. In an attempt to retain more customers, the company can either expect to lower its prices to be more local-consumer friendly or to provide more value to its American patrons through its complimentary services.

To succeed in overseas markets, HaiDiLao needs to gain a comprehensive understanding of its target markets. HaiDiLao is strengthening its products by offering locally grown items. The flavors will reflect more local preferences and flavors. This strategy should attract the American consumer who is used to eating fast food and "bowling alone." HaiDiLao will take their habit of eating alone into account by offering small one-person pots, perhaps at the expense of an authentic, communal Chinese hotpot experience. Some people may argue that HaiDiLao's Initial Public Offering (IPO) value is a bit high. It took place on September 26, 2018 and initially got the price at $2.27 per share, giving it a valuation of about $12 billion. But if the demand is strong and the company is able to appeal to the American consumer, HaiDiLao will gain more deal size and American patrons willing to invest. As the Chinese proverb goes, "There are a thousand Hamlets in a thousand people's eyes." There also can be a thousand hotpots in a thousand people's mouths.

• "No Hostilities Yet"

When nations declare adversity onto each other, there is a lapse of time between the declaration of intention and commencement of hostilities. Implementation can take anywhere from months to years. The Brexit discussions are a major example of such conditions. Code yellow conditions are now in place between Europe and Britain. My wife and I visited England to explore the current and future status.

Evensong in Canterbury Cathedral, seat of the archbishop, is very British, well-attended, firm, strong, and uplifting. There are definite advantages to singing one's prayers. The British production of Jersey Boys was another listening adventure, packed house, lots of fun, energetic singing done well. In London, no signs of fear or concern. St. Martins in the Field did not disappoint with renditions of Mozart at candlelight by a Russian pianist. Trafalgar square was humming and buzzing late into the night as usual. Sticking together while exercising simple precautions is the watchword.

High tea at Harrods was a pleasant experience—but with a twist! Queen Victoria era tea strainers still capture leaves and uplift the taste. The servers in the tea room are sons and daughters of EU nationality, hailing from Hungary, Romania, Estonia, Albania, and Bulgaria. The clientele is mostly Asian.

Vast sums from abroad are being spent at the store—often supported by personal shoppers so that the customer can rapidly move from Hermes to Gucci. That many prices doubled in the past three years seems not to matter. Newspapers report that some of the more intense shoppers purchase more than $2 million of goods per month in one department store alone, supported by the appropriate credit cards Bank Al-Ahly from Egypt, or Union Pay from China. Support also offers inside mosques for prayer services.

All local spenders can forget about the doorman calling a taxi for them! The crowds are massive, all walking on the right—which is the wrong—side, indicating that hardly anyone is British. Multilingual store staff tells us that China is the main country of origin. Russians are left in the wake. Maybe the sanctions are working!

The diversity of restaurants has greatly increased. No longer are there just simple choices between British kidney pies and Indian basmati rice. Still, a shame that the Chinese chain HaiDiLao, with all its hype on quality and service, has yet to open in the United Kingdom.

Uber is very active so one is no longer dependent on the famous and often not appearing taxi.

Drivers are not happy because their income decreased. Still, they do not go to places where customers might naturally congregate, like evening performance conclusions at the Royal Albert Hall. Their argument: What if there are no customers? Hard to argue!

Universities, particularly the mid-grade ones, experience enrollment declines. Costs for non-EU students have skyrocketed. The many students from abroad are mostly bonding and banding among their own nationalities and encounter limited social linkages with Britons. Though internationally oriented, it is quite difficult at many institutions to study or write dissertations in a non-English language.

News and discussions have become less interested in the United States or Europe. On October 3, there was more highlight of the Day of the Open Mosque, than of German reunification day.

There are many changes, some subtle, some not so much. The English gardens hidden from the street are still beautifully tended and restful. And when eating, there are still vast pots of delicious clotted cream. Faucets, newly installed, still separate hot and cold water, no mixing allowed!

So much for flexibility, adjustment, and stability. Conditions are not grim. Historically, one may think of Hannibal's closing onto Italy, with Roman defeat highly likely. But it did not happen in 216 BC and may well not happen in 2019. In spite of signed documents and grim postulations, there is no commencement of hostilities yet. One could label the current conditions as that of the head-burying ostrich, but for now, the feeling is good and the living is easy.

- "Olympics Versus Super Bowl. The Marketing Differences" with Charles Skuba

The Super Bowl reached viewers around the world, but Olympic advertisers will be communicating with a much broader audience from diverse cultures who will bring with them a different set of interests and emotions. To persuade such a multicultural audience, advertising will need to seek commonalities of the mind and heart. Global advertising agencies have the expertise to create messages that work across borders and avoid the danger of leaving broad groups of viewers bewildered or, worse, offended.

We offer five winning techniques (not exclusive to each other) for creative messaging to global audiences during the Olympics in national and global media campaigns.

Universal human emotions come first. The best brands inspire and capture positive, if not joyful, emotion in their customers. Marketers know that emotion often trumps reason in purchase decisions. Dig deep into any customer psyche, whether of a business decision maker or a teenage gamer, and you'll find a bundle of emotions that are common to people across cultures. Although there are cultural differences in what stirs emotion, some things are universal, like love stories and the pursuit of dreams.

For the 2012 London Olympic Games, P&G launched the global "Thank You Mom" campaign that celebrated the love of young Olympic athletes and their mothers. There may be no more powerful bond than the love between a mom and her child and that love is a universal emotion, which is why P&G has renewed the theme for 2018.

Expansive imagery is also of major impact. The film industry has conditioned viewers across the world to crave dramatic, expansive imagery. The most successful global films create a powerful impact of sight and sound. The Olympics are a key opportunity for grand imagery. Marketers regularly use striking visuals to capture attention but the bar is being raised.

Inspiring sounds and music follow hand-in-hand with expansive imagery. Music enhances visuals for dramatic and emotional impact. Marketers must be careful with music selection. Coca-Cola has long used "happiness" music to appeal to young people around the world. Naturally, if the music is great, people will want to share it.

Then there is symbolism. For simple communication of an idea, it's hard to beat. Marketers often employ symbolism to enhance and distinguish their campaign and product messaging.

If you can show product advantage in advertising, your marketing effort is working. The trick is to get people's attention to your message and also sell. Also, marketers would be smart to walk away from messaging that depends upon slang or references to national pop culture.If you didn't grow up watching American television, you might not understand a lot of pop culture references that U.S. audiences instantly absorb.

Super Bowl advertising is uniquely tuned to American audiences, while that of the Olympics must be globally focused. Both will employ many of the techniques identified here. Marketers are literally going for the global gold. For the audience, the Olympic marketing messages will be quite different from the ones of the Super Bowl but well worth waiting for.

- "The Spring Break"

This spring, I wanted my students to remember their "Marketing Across Borders" class, while they traveled to azure beaches and Caribbean getaways. They were to connect their break experiences to some of the themes we have explored in class. Their responses offered an interesting— and illuminating—glimpse into how international marketing shapes the decisions of young travelers.

As digital natives, most of my students performed the research and planning for their trips online. Whether scoring cheaper flights or finding top restaurants, these young travelers turned to social media platforms and travel websites such as AirBnb and TripAdvisor, to find affordable, and often all-inclusive, deals for hotels and flights. Students noted the power of word of mouth, which they far preferred over mass-market pamphlets, in guiding travel decisions. Much trust was placed in the reviews of peer travelers.

Much international travel was to Mexico, the Dominican Republic, and Germany.

But even when my students ventured outside their comfort zones, they still encountered elements of the familiar. They noted the preva- lence of Japanese manufactured cars, such as Toyota, in countries like Mexico and Jamaica. For food, they found a preponderance of American brands—such as McDonalds and Starbucks—that were almost identical to those in Cincinnati, Ohio.

A student, involved in a social justice immersion trip to Jamaica, found international marketing to be an important tool in business development. She found billboards with emotional global brand messages: "Kakoo loves Pepsi!"; "Jamaica, land we love; Honda, car we love." Many messages were targeted toward tourists and rendered in English rather than local languages.

In terms of favorite topics, many of my students' broached food. There was a fascination with the globalization of food products. Students were delighted to taste the delicious meals of the world. "Food trends from around the world had penetrated the Costa Rican market: Breakfast places were serving cold brewed ice coffee, kombucha, acai bowls, avocado toast, and homemade vegan bread. Australians own the best taco joint in Tamarindo. A woman from Minnesota was the chef at a local breakfast café. Markets served poke bowls (sushi bowls from Hawaii), arepas (shredded beef sandwiches from Venezuela), and traditional French pastries."

Students saw a choice of goods that were produced in the United States but tasted differently abroad. In the Dominican Republic, there were different taste versions of Coca Cola. Snacks of choice, such as Doritos, were sold at two different prices depending on whether they were sold in American or Mexican packaging. In Puerto Vallarta, Mexico, the point of sale changed in supermarkets. Oreos were sold alongside American cereals rather than in the cookie section!

All these observations contribute to a wider understanding of international marketing forces that shape tourism for young travelers today. Travel can be good—it gives more perspective, more context, and more variety. Surely, there will be more alternatives and new experiences, which make life more meaningful, spicy, and more interesting.

- "For Want of a Plane"

High hopes were placed into the G20 meeting in Buenos Aires. After all, many policy leaders with different voices were present. In particular, German Chancellor Merkel's role as a seeker of compromise was fully scripted. She was to assure low tariff levels for cars with President Trump, broach new approaches for debt management with Argentina, and discuss issues on Ukraine with President Putin. Alas, the expected discussions were disrupted. The Chancellor's ride did not get there.

When Mrs. Merkel departed Germany, all plans seemed to be on track. Cabinet members, the German Foreign Service team, and a gaggle of journalists had moderately filled the Chancellor's official airplane. But after only 1 of 13 hours of flight time the machine had to turn around for an unplanned landing. Communication was on the fritz, gas could not be ditched, and the subsequent landing back in Cologne/Bonn was heavy. Harsh as it sounds, parked planes don't fly.

Minor inconveniences say you. In an era when the CEO of a declining U.S. multinational firm like GE's Jeff Immelt always had a back-up plane accompany him, surely all the German Air Force had to do was roll out the spare and fly on. Perish the thought! There was a back-up plane. But it had taken off homeward bound for budget reasons once the main trip seemed on track. Also, the spare crew could not perform within regulation time limits.

The German airline Lufthansa was all out of planes for trips to Argentina. Only the Spanish airline Iberia had a direct hop out of Madrid. Not all passengers were excited when their quite empty cabin was suddenly filled up by bureaucrats and guards. Yet others reported that Mrs. Merkel was quiet, focused, and smiling for selfies.

Wagging tongues have suggested that, in light of the harsh electoral decline of her party, Mrs. Merkel wanted to get reacquainted with more popular forms of transportation. Others wonder what Germany's founding Chancellor Bismarck or, worse yet, what President Trump would have said to this failure. Perhaps the lack of a plane tosses Germany, or even the entire European Union into political turmoil.

The problem is not the short-term direct effects, but rather the long-term repercussion that paints reality. How effective are international marketing slogans and expectations emphasizing progress and technology, when the country leader's plane won't fly and airports won't operate? What happens to the brand value of time when a key leader arrives half a day late? How can one be a useful arbiter while not on location? And all this happened just when CEBIT, one of Germany's largest trade fairs for technology and communication, had to close down. Is all this witness to a transition away from leadership struts to execution missteps?

The German aircraft debacle is of major import and impact. Mrs. Merkel may have become more forgiving to her staff. But even though she nods and smiles more, her partners in international discussions take delays very seriously. For them, late is late, which greatly undermines efficiency.

As to President Trump's perspective on these events, he may worry less than expected. First, the problems reaffirm his demand for a substantial increase in European spending on defense. Of equal importance: why should he care about the quality of German planes—he has his own and they fly.

- "The Bear without the Bull"

There is often a strong desire for partisanship both in our domestic and global thinking. Russia keeps being framed as our most vile adversary. Such thinking has much historic background. Of particular worry has been competition in technology—one can still recall the Russian leadership reputation effects of the space launches of Sputnik, the electric ball, and Laika, the spaceship dog. It took the successful North Pole transit of the U.S. submarine Nautilus to re-declare American advantage.

My research in the Georgetown archives yields evidence that not all Russians are adversaries all the time. One example comes from the Russian years of Georgetown University and the Jesuit religious order, which founded it.

The order was initiated by Ignatius of Loyola in Paris in 1534, with its members taking vows of poverty, chastity, and an ode of full obedience to the pope. Its principles and their execution turned out to be quite successful, particularly in the field of education. With its headquarters in Rome, the proximity to the pope helped global expansion and influence.

However, not all was smooth sailing. In spite, or because of their success, the more than 22,000 Jesuits were suppressed in 1773 of all people, by their main patron, Pope Clement XIV. This leader of global Catholicism sent out specific instructions called a "papal bull" or edict to other heads of country, demanding the abolishment of the Jesuit order. The major ruling nations such as the Portuguese and Spanish empires, the French nation, and Austria/Hungary accepted such abolishment, making the Jesuits virtually extinct. Virtually, but not totally, thanks to Russian policy.

At the time, Catherine the Great was the Tsarina or Sovereign of Russia and the protector of its orthodox religion. One of her key objectives was to bring Russia and herself as an equal partner to the table of international leaders. She recognized that raising the capabilities of the Russian population and its nobility to reason and analyze was an important foundation for such an achievement. She was further impressed with the manifold educational activities, which the Jesuits had already set in place. So she was not feeling exploited when the Jesuits requested that the impending papal bull should not arrive or be read by the Imperial Court. She also agreed that existing Jesuits could select Russia as their central headquarters and even allowed them to expand the order.

As a result, those Jesuits, which had been part of the Maryland province in Baltimore, all became Russian in their affiliation, as did their institutions. This relationship remained until 1814 when Pope Pius VII removed the onerous order of suppression. Georgetown University and its Jesuit faculty then became American again.

The lessons learned for today:

- Political hardships imposed to totally eliminate one's adversary may not have to be final—there often is a workaround.
- An international orientation can often be crucial to advancing one's agenda.

- Adversaries and traditions do not have to remain steady and immutable; to the contrary, a new perspective should be raised in one's analysis of conditions.
- Global strengths and unique expertise can set a player apart and permit quite unexpected alliances and cross-references.

The evidence indicates that all this was good for both Russia and Georgetown University. Might there be other strategic linkages possible? It is necessary to separate the bear from the bull and to remember that there is always a bear market somewhere.

CHAPTER 3

Relationships With New Technology

- "Technology: a Key Catalyst in a Changing Society"

When analyzing the midterm COVID-19 effects, many pundits envision a return to the status quo ante once the current societal disruptions have calmed down. We doubt such an outcome due to the magnitude of the societal shifts triggered by COVID-19 along with the emergence of new technologies that take on an increasingly important role for business, government, and the individual. Just like toothpaste once squeezed out of the tube becomes difficult to repackage back into the tube, policy and behavior once explored become very challenging to ignore.

Technology is today's most critical man-made driver of global shifts, replacing and substituting established processes. It has already renewed content and context for many firms and individuals. For example, new routings between countries and consumers that were traditionally impassable or leading to long time delays have been made accessible, thus creating what some have called a death (or at least diminishment) of distance. The opening of the Swiss Ceneri base tunnel provides greatly enhanced connectivity between Alpine mountain ranges. The Zhuhai Bridge makes a dramatic new connection to Hong Kong, Macau, and Mainland China. Both of these edifices have changed geographic proximity.

Owing to technology, information can now be rapidly transferred around the globe. While immigration may be fueling population shifts in wealthy nations, technology is fueling the growth of the business and consumption flows around the world. Historically, worker mobility was a critical human resource variable that involved changing physical presence. Today, worker mobility may mean as little as someone working on a computer at a different location. Increasingly, there is no longer even the need for such activity to take place synchronously.

The power of technology can be momentous and its impact may not always be fully visible from the start of its implementation. Often its relevance bubbles under the surface. A testament to the importance of technology is broadband Internet. As an indicator of technological development, the number of fixed broadband subscribers matters since a high number of subscribers per capita usually indicates a high level of technology. Advanced economies tend to have the most broadband subscribers, which is most reflective of business capabilities. By contrast, the number of subscribers in many developing economies, such as Burkina Faso and Afghanistan, is currently effectively zero. Thus, technologies tend to be most evolved in advanced economies and least evolved in developing economies. The distinction is important because technology is critical to entrepreneurship, productivity, innovation, national economic vitality, and superior living standards.

Technological developments over the past decade have led to dramatic changes in the way people think about communication and information sharing. Mobile telephone subscriptions worldwide keep rising greatly and contribute the largest share of worldwide sales in the consumer electronics sector. Many mature markets have over 100 percent mobile penetration (meaning that some owners have more than one phone, not that all members of that market's population own a phone).

Technological advances lead to greater information sharing worldwide and allow for new equipment to be more sophisticated and perform more functions at a lower cost. More intelligent and accurate control equipment can bring energy efficiency and large cost savings. As we look at the world marketplace, our planning should focus more on technology. With more technology, even poor countries can become more efficient and successful. Enhanced with the power of financial remittances and acquisition of innovation from countries around the world, technology should become the watchword for the future.

- "America, Germany, and Hungary: A New Relationship"

With the U.S. presidential election coming up, along with so many other uncertainties, it is important now more than ever to look to what the future may hold. Those with insight toward a future that is still internationally connected are increasingly important.

Interesting times bring continuous changes, which in turn affect national linkages and alliances. A pre-eminent example is the relationship between the United States, Germany, and Hungary.

Take the German domestic diversity. By comparison with the United States, Germans have had very limited exposure to Africans. Only after major migration waves, does diversity permeate society more—yet there is very little official activity providing support to People of Color.

Take the use of words: the term "race" in the German Constitution is seen, after more than 70 years, as troublesome, since it tends to imply discrimination. A substitution of the term is part of a major national debate instead of an ongoing threat from the coronavirus.

Of concern to the reader is the lack of public German encouragement for the "pursuit of happiness." This admonition that is so aptly reflected in the American Declaration of Independence is of major significance. Citizens of Germany should acknowledge and accept that directions for a citizen's life path should not only consist of admonitions to work but also include the opportunity for enjoyment, which the United States has in its "pursuit of happiness," encoded in its Declaration of Independence.

The United States has problems, some of them major ones. In consequence, Europeans, particularly Germans, hasten to draw conclusions about European superiority. The jocular aspects are so profound that, as one can discover, there is not even room for debate. The United States (and its president, government, policies, and ambassador) are said to be just plain wrong, that's all there is to it—from a European, and particularly German perspective.

Statements about U.S. policy makes life disconcerted. For example, President Trump announced the withdrawal of U.S. troops from Germany. Why exuberantly protect Germany with U.S. forces when a long promised 2 percent German contribution to its military budgets had not been delivered? There was an uproar in Germany designating Americans as derogatory merchants only preoccupied with money. No comparison was made to much earlier visits by Ronald Reagan's Secretary of the Treasury Jim Baker who, tin cup in hand traversed Europe with the slogan "feed, fund, or fight," thus stressing participation while giving every ally viable options. Even less was mentioned about commitments made and or kept. Nothing was heard about the fact that military payment of 2 percent of GDP represents an investment, not some wild and senseless expenditure.

Fascinating are the intra-European comparisons of nations, many of which have found their orbit around Germany. Concessions in one field then trigger sacrifices in another. For example, in many German rankings, Poland is relatively low. However, their help in bringing in the German asparagus harvest works as an important redeeming factor. For many Germans, the import of agricultural products has tended to be unimportant. However, after the renewed COVID-19 outburst in their key domestic butchering plant, procurement from abroad suddenly gained important priority.

How do these changes refurbish internal alliances? My bets are on Hungary. That country has, more often than not, hit rock bottom due to invasions but has always recouped, even though it sometimes did take much time. Some controversies surrounding Hungary exist. Just the other day I overheard a German parliamentarian comment, warning that some legislation would lead to Hungarian conditions in Germany. That did not appear in the friendly way of consuming kolbasz, Tokaji wine, or palinka, but rather a derogatory statement. Amazing it is, in light of many Hungarian Nobel prizes, toy, and machinery production. Also, one might not forget the 1989 opening of the Hungarian border to Germans by the Hungarian Foreign Secretary Gyula Horn who effectively set the stage for German unification.

Hungarians have always, in history, experienced the friction of being caught between East and West. Going back to the hordes of Mongols, Huns, and even Austrians, the country has been decimated. Nonetheless, there was consistency in Hungary's desire to adhere to the West of Europe. Nowadays, Hungary takes on repeated leadership positions when it comes to policy design and implementation. Its management of immigration flows has, over time, been adapted by other European nations. Its acceptance of marketing principles for its society leaves much room for other Europeans to learn. The pricing policies of stores and services continue to be reasonable. But whenever Hungary initiates an innovation, the rest of Europe claims to suffer. Credit for Hungarian progress is only rarely given. Almost similar to the United States now.

Over time, relationships change for both internal and external reasons. Take the U.S./UK relations, which were always categorized as a special linkage between the two countries. Yet, the relationship is not quite the same anymore, particularly since Britain has left the European Union. Germany has its own set of problems. Many of its policies no longer reflect a firm economic and policy friendship with the United States. When relationships between nations have more to offer each other, they will result in actions that strengthen each nation's competitiveness.

- "Dealing with Disruptive Dislocations"

The third installment of pieces focusing on coronavirus and its effects on international business, this piece compares currency risk sharing with COVID-19, offering a unique and interesting comparison to be found. Here we go:

The coronavirus disruption intensifies. Questions of human safety and business continuity reach far beyond lock-down orders. What can be done to manage the unexpected? Are there analog situations of help, recourse, and guidance? This commentary is based on some

well-developed theories of international business, which might be use-
fully applied to COVID-19 transmissions.

One virus comparison can come from currency risk management.
COVID-19 is more deadly, but its frequency and strength vary at different
times and locations. For currencies, companies share and trade-off risk
with their partners to reduce the effects of dislocations. A similar approach
works for health care. Ventilators and testing capabilities may at one time
be needed more in one region than in another. Together with hospital
beds they can be shipped to hot spots. Even medical personnel can be
transferred around the globe to cope with imbalances. When needs shift,
return shipments can be administered fairly.

Firms that continuously trade have ongoing economic currency
exposure. Typically, such firms wish to maintain good relationships with
their business partners. Good partners between suppliers and customers
do not force all the currency risk of international transactions onto the
business partner. Both currency and viral risks have a good portion of
randomness to them. In the finance sector, risk-sharing agreements have
proven to be useful under such conditions.

Here is an example with companies A (American) and B (Israeli),
both multinationals. If A continuously trades with B and pays in New
Shekel, then major swings in currency values may cause one party to
benefit at the expense of the other. Firms can address such a problem with
currency management.

Both companies could agree that all purchases by A will be made in
Israeli New Shekel, as long as the currency value on the payment date
(spot rate) remains between 0.25 and 0.3 New Shekel/$. Such range
lets A agree to accept any currency exposure because it is paying in the
foreign currency. If, however, the exchange rate falls outside of this range
on the payment date, A and B will "share" the difference. If the spot rate
is 0.35 New Shekel/$, then the Israeli currency would have depreciated.
Because this rate would fall outside of the contractual range, a sharing
arrangement would divide up the shift between the parties. Therefore,
B loses 0.05 New Shekel/$, and A gains 0.05 New Shekel/$. Not ideal,
but long-term preferable to each party absorbing its own full exchange
rate impact.

Such risk-sharing agreements have been in use for nearly 50 years in
modern world markets. They became something of a rarity during the

1950s and 1960s when exchange rates were relatively stable under the Bretton Woods Agreement. Firms with long-term customer/supplier relationships across borders can now return to some old ways of keeping old friends; since it synchronizes imbalances and eases adjustment intensities.

- "International Data Need to Add Up"

A useful analysis requires the understanding of data and a belief both in the data and their issuer. Companies, organizations, and scholars vary widely in their interpretation and use. International comparisons often differ substantially in data collection and quality control. This commentary eases comparisons of research across national borders. Here is an international perspective on research numbers, going beyond quantitative data aspects and embedding human warmth and insights.

In an era of lengthy and diverse supply chains, investors need to transparently identify corporate action and its effect on the market place. Clear rules of origin are just like license plates. They identify ownership and assign responsibility. Labels cannot simply state "manufactured in the European Union."

Information needs to be compatible across domains. For example, to compare medical information across nations, one has to segment patient differences by age, country, health patterns, and variations in the access to medical care, prophylactic treatment, and pharmaceuticals.

Culture affects personal behavior. For example, research identified the wearing of face masks helpful to viral containment. In Asia, there was ongoing and rapid use of breathing masks. Particularly in wintertime, masks were encouraged both to protect oneself and others from contamination. No negative connotation is associated with the use of a mask. By contrast, in the United States, a mask reflects for many the existence of a medical problem by the wearer. In consequence, masks are not seen as protective but rather as an announcer of risk, which in turn negates their use.

Social structure matters, particularly as it reflects differences in infrastructure and trust. Not all countries have the capability to fund and collect data within short time spans. The need to save face can then lead to the furnishing of poor data, delivered with elan. In consequence, "current" information may really be old and may not even begin to alert users to important changes in one's society or social conditions.

Data work needs to recognize the emotional component of information. How will people feel about their direct exposure to hard and cold numbers alone? How can one systematically but honestly include emotions into one's analysis? How to cope with self-fulfilling prophecies? What are the short- and long-term effects of optimism with data—particularly when insights can cover the entire range of a scale? For most people, numbers are mere indicators of opportunities for action and change.

Analyses and forecasts need to consider change. An evaluation based on the next quarter may reflect the next 25 years. Insufficient or incorrect reflection of change and innovation may lead to precariously wrong decisions. Imagine the decision-making process for countertrade, where the outcome and conclusion of an agreement may take decades.

Synchronicity is another important dimension. I am reminded of Ludwig Erhard, the second chancellor of the Federal Republic of Germany who was credited with Germany's postwar "Wirtschaftswunder" or economic miracle. When Erhard concentrated expenditures on some sectors and called for a "tightening of belts" for others, these steps were rapidly and fully implemented by government, firms, and society, leading to a powerful impact. The players actually cared.

On this dimension, President Biden will find his largest risk and opportunity. The coordinated development of a restructured economy accompanied by a synchronous response of all participants with their resources can turn into a wonderful economy that shakes off the problems of post coronavirus rebuilding like a duck shakes off water.

Apart from human emotions, economic re-emergence requires measurement scales benefiting from recalibration and new benchmarks. For example, a scale measuring export controls, which ranges from "no controls" to "tight controls," is only in part complete since it omits policy resulting from subsidies and voluntary restraints. Numbers are only snapshots of a current condition. These conditions are not frozen in salt, but they will change and with them their impact. In a dynamic and complex environment, even the efficacy of Aspirin benefits from review.

- "Services: Performance of the Future"

Services have outperformed the economic leverage of manufacturing. The growth not only changes the structure and composition of economic activities in both the United States and the world but also leads to a more integrated future. Both legislators and negotiators must pay more attention to the service components of international exchanges if they are to achieve long-term change.

Worldwide, services contributed more than 60 percent of total value added in most major economies in 2017. China and India were the exceptions. For world trade, the value of services exports grew 5.1 percent per year between 2006 and 2016 with a rising tendency.

U.S. services now account for over two-thirds of GDP. The U.S. companies achieved more than $2.2 trillion in recorded international services sales. In trade, services deliver a large surplus. Four out of five new private-sector jobs in the United States are created by services. In 2015, the Peterson Institute estimated that the elimination of global barriers to trade in services would increase the U.S. service exports by $300 billion and create 3 million jobs when fully implemented.

There is more to services than meets the eye. Services come in different categories and at different, often opaque international levels. Examples are varied performances in fields such as telecommunications, financial services, computer services, retail distribution, environmental services, education, and express delivery.

Manufacturing strength increasingly comes from strong and tailor-made services, which enable manufacturing to be more effective and competitive. Current cars are service driven and updated with sophisticated navigation systems. TVs have to connect to streams in order to be smart. iPhone sales rely on Apple's support services, including troubleshooting and retailing. Even a traditional aerospace exporter like Boeing uses cloud services to manage inventory, optimize maintenance, and minimize the costs of system malfunctions.

Service performance at high has typically been greatly underestimated due to insufficient measurement insight. For example, if a person travels abroad for medical tourism, such value generating activity is hardly recorded. A local session of advice with a financial expert may create high value. However, poor valuation and insufficient recordation lead to only little understanding of current account impact.

Services and manufacturing are not at opposite ends of a scale. Rather, services strengthen the performance of manufacturing and are enhanced by the application of technology. Through its investment in the services sector, China has greatly improved the capabilities of its logistics, transport, and infrastructure conditions. China can now demonstrably use its newly generated logistics expertise to outperform its competitors. For example, due to its service investments, the transport time of persons and goods via the new Hong Kong–Zhuhai–Macao Bridge has diminished from 4 hours to 30 minutes since the end of 2018. What a time warp, yielding clear insights into shifting capabilities. Many will be the companies and countries that sign up to exchange raw materials for infrastructure.

The integration between services and manufacturing will relegate entire supply chain conditions, which have been laboriously created, to a mere blur. Today, most apparel manufacturers own retail stores. Many store brands like Target build up their own manufacturing, controls, and retail distribution. Apple manufactures its own chips, fingerprint sensors, and other custom components. Concurrently, its retail stores flourish and allow it to control its direct distribution and sale to customers.

Services growth promotes new types of manufacturing. Printing technology gives new meaning to scale economies. Services, combined with flexibility and adjustment, bring opportunity and vitality to the global economy. In terms of innovation and employment, strong services are no less important for a country than a strong manufacturing sector. U.S. legislators and negotiators must place growing emphasis on services and their links, both direct and indirect, with manufacturing. A more integrated economy will provide all with a significant payoff.

- "History does not always tell the Future" with Michael Lukas

Historically, increased international trade activities are often linked to the growth of a country. National power in the world was often the result of creating new markets and trade. For example, the Roman Empire achieved immense growth through the linkages of business rather than the marching of legions and warfare. Many economic successes also occurred when previously closed economies embraced international trade like South Korea in 1960s and China in 1980s.

So far, in this century, more than a billion people around the world have been lifted out of poverty by the power of international trade. International competition has greatly stimulated innovation and productivity.

However, world trade is in flux today. Conflicts have emerged over market instabilities and insecure trade structures, which have led to major inequities. No longer are societies certain that an increase in trade resolves current economic and societal shortcomings. Will a better life result from simply doing more of what was done in the past?

Globally, some policy makers intend to ride inequities to the hilt. They give preference to the continuity of rules over the adjustment to reality. For them tradition is the overriding decision tool.

But, what happens when the fundament has changed? When a volcano erupts and sends a stream of glowing lava flowing down the mountain, the affected villages are no longer fit for shelter. Today, President Trump reflects the need for new actions in a new era. He is positively willing to disregard the past when its performance distorts the playing field. The consequences have been important.

In 2017, the United States started to renegotiate its trade agreements with Canada, Mexico, and South Korea. It questions the World Trade Organization (WTO) and challenges the whole trade administration system. In addition, a series of import tariffs came into effect. All these steps indicate a better understanding of shortcomings in trade and a quick-footed willingness to precipitate a curative impact. President Reagan already indicated that "all politics are local." That principle is expanded into a new approach that states "timing matters for change."

Continuing large trade imbalances and growing foreign investment control are sources of dissatisfaction. Domestic producers fear to be squeezed by global rivals. New production technology, such as product printing, makes manufacturing history obsolete. Processes also matter. China has taken full advantage of the trade infrastructure built by the United States and the European Union only to subsequently challenge the status quo. The United States's share of world exports has declined precipitously from 25 percent in the 1950s to less than 9 percent in 2017. The U.S. share of world imports now accounts for 13 percent of world imports. When compared to its exports, the United States clearly has an excess import consumption.

Reshaping a global system is tough work. Since 1945, the United States has been at the center of the global economy. In its competition with the socialist system, market orientation has clearly been won by America.

Encouraging other nations to help guide the world to better lives does not represent an abdication of leadership. The United States's willingness to let others participate in the design and implementation of crucial adjustments demonstrates a willingness to permit others to learn, an encouragement of self-determination, and a great spirit of security and comfort with change.

The debates over international trade might rumble on for years. But we already know that trade policy must become more domestically oriented, while domestic policy must become more international in vision. Doing so, must shape the future.

- "The Case for Cuban Engagement"

After six decades of communist rule in Cuba, the island is now governed by someone outside of the Castro family for the first time since the 1959 revolution. The new leader, Miguel Diaz-Canel, was vice president and a provincial party chief.

Many believe that the political and economic status quo of the Caribbean nation is unlikely to change. However, lessons from the business world indicate that any change in an organization's key leaders ushers in a new era for a company.

Whether it's an acquisition, merger, or the appointment of a new CEO, these transformations usually carry enormous repercussions for key functions.

New priorities are typically manifested by new promotions, new players, new rules, and new aims. In turn, this results in shifting financial conditions, new private developments, and new service assortments.

When applying such transition effects onto countries, one could argue that there is an opportunity for President Biden to act decisively in formalizing and normalizing trade relations with Cuba if conciliatory and meaningful changes are made.

For example, changes could be made so that there are no longer higher hotel rates for Americans than for Europeans, as well as no more ongoing accusations or regurgitation of historic events that have long passed.

Curative International Marketing, a theory developed at Georgetown University's McDonough School of Business, directly addresses past errors and focuses on long-term restitution and improvements.

Such a move would advance U.S. businesses and their strategic interests, while allowing Cuban citizens to operate in the private sector independent of the communist regime.

So far in the Trump administration, the opposite tactic has been taken by restricting American travel and trade with Cuba, which was a reversal of President Barack Obama's policies.

A pro-business posture allows for increased commercial relations (beyond cigars) that would be more effective in countering the interests of the Cuban military's monopoly in business.

This policy would empower private Cuban entrepreneurs by eliminating their dependence on the Cuban state apparatus and open them up to U.S. leadership and influence in the region. Private success over public ventures would speak volumes in favor of new economic and social thinking.

As a first measure, restoring the capacity for U.S. citizens to schedule individual visits to Cuba, which was eliminated in 2017, should be considered.

The potential economic boon for Cuba's tourist industry could eventually stimulate growth in both the U.S. and Cuban economies. Also, this measure would promote democratization and bolster innovation and an entrepreneurial spirit in Cuba.

The recent promising developments in the Korean Peninsula indicate that diplomacy rather than deterrence can advance American interests in places where ideological and strategic divisions run deep. As the White House approaches a deal in East Asia, it could apply the lessons learned from the North Korean negotiations closer to home in Cuba.

Cuba represents an important task in aligning economic dimensions. Opening conversations—and trade—with the island could mark a vast improvement in the bilateral relationship. Hopefully, the American people can look forward to the use of politics that shapes a future good for all of us.

- "Douse The Wildfires"

Public information should be both accurate and interesting. When there is a conflict between the two, many information users prefer an outcome based on truth. Lately, there have been growing scandals that taint media considered traditionally to be of quality.

Some believe that this is a problem only encountered by President Trump or the United States. Far from it, we are not alone! From around the world, one learns about misdirections and shortfalls in media accuracy. For example, late last year the German magazine *Der Spiegel* had to admit that its key investigative reporter, Mr. Claas Relotius, had plainly fabricated stories in many of his articles over the past seven years. The individuals he described or allegedly interviewed either did not exist or had not made the attributed statements. Relationships were mischaracterized and the context reported was either falsely described or nonexistent.

As the most important information source for many users, the media must take responsibility for the ethical and honorable delivery of fact-based and reliable messages. The opportunity is there. New information-gathering capabilities can be a tool to improve quality.

Continuing poor work will further erode the public information space. For example, one can easily imagine a land without newspapers. Already, their role in the wrapping of fishes has been severely diminished.

The issue is of particularly great importance to the global investment community. Poor information leads to increased uncertainty and risk. In 2013, stock markets lost $130 billion in two minutes after the Associated Press posted false news about an explosion in the White House that was said to have injured President Obama. In the same year, the Chinese construction company Zoomlion's share price tumbled 26.9 percent on the Hong Kong stock exchange when the state-owned CCTV network published a series of fake stories by a corrupted reporter.

For individual investors, wrong news will hurt their confidence in products or companies, which they might use or invest. In consequence, lack of investment may lead to great opportunities missed.

In the long run, people have to learn, absorb, understand, and react to surprising political results or sudden economic unrest. Life will continue to present spectacular events such as the 2016 U.S. presidential election or Brexit, which can lead to confusing flows of information. Cross-national effects can be triggered by national inaccuracies. In German's

"Spiegelgate," fake pieces largely focused on U.S. policies and segments of the American population. There were stories about U.S.–Mexican border conflicts with made-up "Mexicans Keep Out" signs, which may have intensified local disagreements.

Media worldwide need to regain public trust. Fact-checking must be improved. Credibility requires more transparency and a greater indication of global linkages. Also, the tasks of gathering and distribution should be viewed with appropriate humility.

It will be difficult for media, both old and emerging, to maintain and rebuild credibility. When key politicians tweet about an informational heap of bovine waste, they reflect the risk of a decline comparable to that of the typewriter or medical application of leeches. Media need a commitment to honesty, accountability, transparency, and personal responsibility, also for its global communication, in order to offer a safe and reliable public information space.

- "The Ignorant Wise Man"

American companies were assured that because of its size and the diversity of its resources, the American economy could satisfy consumer wants and national needs with a minimal reliance on foreign trade. The availability of a large U.S. domestic consumption power and the relative distance to foreign markets resulted in many U.S. manufacturers simply not feeling a compelling need to seek business beyond national borders. Subsequently, the perception emerged within the private sector that exporting and international marketing were simply too risky, complicated, and not worth it.

This perception also resulted in increasing gaps in international marketing knowledge between managers in the United States and those abroad. This gap shaped different incentives to innovation. The Late-developing Advantage Theory can illustrate those differences, not only at a national but also at a firm specific level. A less favorable position can always be an opportunity and motivation. While business executives who deal with small market sizes are willing to learn about cultural sensitivity and market differences, many U.S. managers remain blissfully ignorant of the global economy. Given such lack of global interest, inadequacy of information, ignorance of where and how to market internationally, unfamiliarity with foreign market conditions, and complicated trade regulations, the U.S. private sector became uninterested and fearful of conducting international business activities.

However, conditions have changed. Traditional education institutions are becoming more attuned to the international dimension. Universities, and particularly business programs, are emphasizing responsibilities and obligations at the international level both in theory and in practice. Meanwhile, some government agencies are paying closer attention to the international needs of the U.S. business community. The U.S. Department of State offers training and instruction in business–government relations to domestic firms.

Newly emerging economies also accelerate the process of rising public attention. For instance, electronic commerce has made it more feasible to reach out to the global business community, whether a firm is large or small. International events can lend a new focus to business. In 2018, Alibaba generated US$30.69 billion in sales on Double Eleven or November 11, which is known as a day of special promotions, and now includes a large share of international sales. Related industries and supply chains, such as transportation and logistics, are prospering with the growing volume of international trade as well.

In effect, U.S. corporate interests given to international markets as an opportunity find both customers and suppliers to be growing. How can the United States maintain a sustainable competitive position? How can the managers further learn from what used to be former students? The need and demand for international marketing expertise can be expected to rise substantially. Overall, avoiding ignorance is the first step to becoming wiser.

• "Package from China: Who pays the freight?"

Running a small business that ships low-weight merchandise, say 10 T-shirts or small hardware from China to the United States, made logistics cost easy. The United States provided for a large shipping discount of 40 percent to 70 percent.

Such generosity came from U.S. membership in the Universal Postal Union (UPU). Founded in 1874, the UPU is the international postal organization in Switzerland, committed to a smoothly running international postal system.

In 1969, the UPU's developed country members implemented discounts for poor nations when shipping small parcels. China then was isolated with few outward shipments. In consequence, consumers in Washington found that the shipping cost of a face cream was more affordable from China than from Los Angeles. Today, however, China delivers more than one billion small packages a year to the United States and the special discount treatment continued.

Then there came change. The Trump Administration announced U.S. withdrawal from the UPU as of October 17, 2018. The objective was to arrive at competitive and fair global shipping rates. This move showed the Trump Administration's willingness to leave and quit multilateral agreements judged unfavorable to U.S. interests. Although the UPU withdrawal process takes one year, U.S. deep discounts for Chinese packages ended immediately.

Now China Post has introduced a new Express Mail Service. It raised the price of packages to the United States from $30 to $34 for the first 0.5 kilogram shipped. Who pays, who benefits?

The United States Postal Service (USPS) can use higher payments from China. But transshipments through other nations and competition will lead to reduced shipping volume.

The price advantage of many Chinese e-commerce vendors declines. Higher cost of shipping reduces this advantage even further. Most endangered are eBay-type international vendors. Sellers who compete on price alone face higher cost and more competition. To survive it will become a new practice to find alternatives for product and service delivery, both for processes as well as markets.

Adjusting the rules for new conditions makes sense. Few parameter conditions have remained static for 144 years. The UPU should get ready for a significant restructuring. What applies to China, the United States, and other relationships, applies to other nations as well. One should expect further exploration of antiquated subsidies, which have been bypassed by new market conditions. Such tracking can identify new opportunities for change and innovation.

De-subsidization will create market alternatives based on new forms of delivery. Such adjustments will be cost analyzed and competitively compared to achieve higher efficiency. Legislators and internationally active framers of distance trade, such as the World Bank and the World Trade Organization can use this opportunity to pinpoint, develop, and scale up models that reflect transport cost-sensitive sectors and practices. In addition to greater accuracy and fairness, the President's initiative for higher prices can lead to higher capabilities, more efficiencies, and better services. A good start!

CHAPTER 4

Curative Marketing Can Cure

- Battling the Virus Strengthens Education with Michael L. Czinkota

The coronavirus is the firing pin for major innovations. In many educational institutions, less than half of the customary study time is invested in this year's academic spring semester. There is some distance learning, but in many instances, the faculty is very much dependent on technology, which they learn from students rather than the traditional reverse flow.

We give you here an article written by two Michael Czinkotas dealing with the same issue: One is professor in the McDonough School of

Business at Georgetown University, the other is the nephew, a student with most experience gathered in Germany. Here we go:

The virus brings rapid innovation to the education industry. Just consider that traditionally, the entire sector has not distinguished itself with high-speed change. A debate on the cost of tuition was strongly buttressed by the biblical anecdote of the young Jesus Christ ejecting the money changers from the temple. That event was two thousand years ago.

In the university sector, if one could implement time travel for professors and their students, they could be safely delivered to a university town and be rapidly functional in their work. There still remains the amphitheater seating of chairs. There is the black or white board to communicate information. There is the professor upfront moving from one room side to the other, while students take notes or raise their hand indicating readiness for comment.

Any changes to this model require approval by at least four faculty committees, each one of which needs substantial time to investigate the potential repercussions of alterations. Then there are reviews by board members, insights from administrators, and the "Fingerspitzengefühl" of financial liaison. Woe the planner of change who is likely to encounter a lead time of lead. The bottom line: Change for education is very difficult and hard to achieve.

How has the education system performed under virus conditions? We can attribute to its very high degrees of rapidity, focus, transparency, and adaptation, which lead to significant changes. Students, by the tens of thousands, are shifting their main residence within a week. Faculty members have at the same time solidified new course materials and given major thought to content delivery under entirely new conditions. Administrators had to rapidly find ways to work with complaining and even incensed students and parents.

How to conduct an international program under conditions of severely inhibited travel? How to interact with high mobility groups? How to adjust the delivery of an excellent classroom joke that now has no classroom audience?

Long-term contemplations must now be considered and decided on with a new kind of time framework—we suggest 10 days for adaption of innovation. A textbook that was developed over 40 years now needs a revision time measured in weeks. The virus has given us a way to cope with complexity using extraordinary speed. There are now innovations that are finally accepted, which pump new energy and strength into the body politic. The best infusion is yet to come.

In Germany, educational changes have been seen as the end of the world. Even students at an airport on a school day were seen as a threat to society for missing out on their classes. Now, due to the virus, students must stay at home. Schools whose mission had gradually shifted from being institutions for learning to offering pressure against drugs, against cigarettes, for democracy, and for diversity. It appears that teachers are now beginning to teach again, and students can ask questions that actually are answered. Although in past events of national need, the ability to adapt resources appeared not to exist, this time, the resources, and the teachers are all here, all in support of insights and service of German youth.

Also, remember, that once for whatever reason, the toothpaste has left the tube, it won't go back in, which leads to totally different uses and expectations. Earlier societies and time periods had their own changes, some without much benefit such as bubonic plague and the great influenza epidemic. Other changes triggered much displacement but led also to eventual improvement to society. Examples are the printing press of Gutenberg, electricity by Edison, and planes by the Wright brothers.

The coronavirus leads to adjustments that result in new approaches, unexpected adaptations, and a much wider field of options. We will have new playing fields, new players, and new rules. The postviral times will not necessarily be convenient or tranquil, but there will be many more opportunities for innovation and creativity. Sometimes it takes a large hurdle to overcome obstacles, but focus and collaboration achieve much progress. This may be a time for a new jointness of purpose.

- "The Coronavirus: A New Risk for Trade"

Over the past three generations, analyses of trade have indicated that speed of innovation and change is supportive of improved living standards. Growth of a country's international trade has typically been more rapid than growth of the domestic economy.

There is strong historic support for the benefit of speed. The Roman Empire's impact on thought and development can still be felt today. Its territories, also in the Middle East, were expanded less through armed conflicts, but rather through the speed and improvements offered to its international collaborators. The Pax Romana insured that merchants could travel safely on the roads that were built, maintained, and protected by Roman legions. The common coinage facilitated the speed of business transactions throughout the empire. Central market locations through the foundation of cities and excellent communication systems enabled the development and distribution of innovations.

But conditions change. On February 02, 2021, the U.S. State Department placed China on a travel advisory of "Level 4: Do Not Travel" due to the novel coronavirus (COVID-19) outbreak. As of February 12, 2021, the death toll from the virus was at least 1,113.

It matters how quickly something can be provided to a specific location. Also needed is control of the speed of distribution combined with the capability to plan for the "what if" question in case a disruption of shipment is required.

We need to discover and systematically assess possible trouble spots of globalization and highlight the consequences of dependence. It is vital for the formulation of strategic visions to understand the need and capacity for disruption.

In the 1970s, Professor Bernard LaLonde of The Ohio State University expanded his analysis of inventory carrying cost to include the expense of capital tied up in the storage of goods. With interest rates of 17 percent and higher during the Carter presidency, his innovative assessment of expense and risk changed corporate inventory management substantially.

The speed of Chinese viral contamination sends us a risk signal for trade. We discover that rapid propagation does not just work for incoming and outgoing goods and services. Just as there has been substantial growth in health care tourism, where patients obtain lower cost medical services by traveling abroad, the expansion of viral infection can be hard to contain.

Rapid distribution outward and inward can be deteriorating and distracting. The coronavirus outbreak is our wakeup call to be alert, not just to the benefits but also the risks encountered in international outflows and inflows of services, ideas, thoughts, and goods.

This problematic concern raises the key issue of how to deal with such risky occurrences. One useful approach is the consultation with experts who have experienced sudden, frequent, and unexpected risk conditions. Such expertise can be sourced best from the Middle East, where there have been many past occurrences of uncertainty, scrutiny, and restraint. Local experts may be able to help manage hostile business environments both at home and abroad. They can anticipate repercussions from disruptions and also calm down hyper reactions. And therein lies much of the wheel of fortune: If enough people believe in a condition, their understanding may well become reality. Let us not accept complex issues without expert insights.

- "Good Souls Bring Curative Marketing"

A good soul promotes quality of humility, empathy, and reflections for human developments at a time when society often perceives business as soulless. Today, concern over the lack of soul in business life creates a fine layer of transparent filigree, which negatively shadows and biases public impressions. Eventual fossilization may turn out to be very costly, since it influences society's willingness to allocate, spend, play, and nudge.

People and society generally seek pursuits, which advance wealth and good feelings. But nowadays, wealth seems to have won out. Concurrently, technology and artificial intelligence may contribute to further alienate business from the soul. The environment appears to weaken the overall qualities of a soul. Two fatal crashes involving Boeing 737 Max 8 planes have faltered public confidence in the aviation giant. Volkswagen's Teutonic attraction to honesty was deflected by its cheating on the emissions of diesel engines. Church child abuse scandal reveals a faith's failure to govern human behavior. All these cases may lead to a separation of business and society, where business becomes a mere supply chain member without influence or respect.

The events are not just contemporaneous. More than a century ago, the Chinese Empress Dowager Tz'u-hsi, in order to renovate her summer palace, impounded government funds that had been designated for China's shipping and its navy. Almost totally isolated from world trade, China missed out on knowledge transfer, the inflow of goods, global innovation, and the productivity growth that derive from international trade.

Passage of time may lead to the forgiveness of misdeeds, but such mercy does not exempt one from recognizing their responsibility. Curative marketing may well be the upcoming direction to restore the good soul by raising wonderment about the triple helix linkage of business, faith, and society.

Business must look back and accept responsibility for past errors. A more emotionally appealing approach, for example, should have been taken by the Boeing Company in recognition of its responsibilities. Merchants should be reliable, trustworthy, and bridge-building partners. For now, American firms, when compared to their global competitors, should strive for a transparent, humble, and discerning leadership.

Since the 1990s, governments again have begun to play a growing role in business. New global regulations and restrictions have emerged, because markets don't always succeed with constraints and self-regulation.

Today, the traditional role and effectiveness of the World Trade Organization are challenged. Multilateral agreements appear to be at a standstill or even in retrenchment. At the same time, the Trump administration's deregulation brings confidence to the domestic economy. A 2018 survey by the National Association of Manufacturers showed that more than 92 percent of respondents suggested a positive outlook for their firms. Nearly a half-million new manufacturing jobs were created in the past two years.

The new and crucial joint responsibility of humanity, business, and faith can and should be used to humanize behavior, expectations, and cultivation. Religious connectivity with commerce has had an important role for ages. There is, for example, the ejection of the money changers from the synagogue by Jesus and the creation of the honorable merchant, developed by the German Hanse Trading Group in the 13th century.

Curative marketing helps overcome past shortcomings and leads to a healthier economy. China, for example, tries to heal past wounds in areas such as food safety, environmental protection, and medical security.

In the preface of my book *In Search for the Soul of International Business*, Dr. Szabo, the Hungarian ambassador to the United States, states that "one of my goals is to strengthen business ties between Hungary and the United States. I would like to see businesses flourish that have multidimensional levels of depth and a natural concern for a good soul so that these connections can be meaningful, long-lasting, and honorable."

Good souls should not only point business to an exchange of human development for profit. Curative marketing should be the next step to help create an environment of global responsibility and growth.

Free Trade Zones and Counterfeit Goods

The European Union Intellectual Property Office (EUIPO) and the Organization for Economic Cooperation and Development (OECD)'s recent report claims that free trade zones (FTZs) may be facilitating illegal activities, such as trade in counterfeit and pirated products, by providing good infrastructure with little oversight over its use.

FTZs encompass a broad range of activities, from tourism to retail sales. They typically represent duty-free customs areas, or offer benefits based on location, in a geographically limited space. Today, there are over 3,500 zones in 130 economies, collectively employing 66 million workers worldwide.

A number of benefits drive countries to embrace FTZs. In general, these areas increase a nation's foreign exchange reserves and improve the balance of payments. On a local level, new supply chains increase business for domestic producers that sell inputs by zone-based firms. Finally, these areas provide jobs that bolster employment and, at least in developing countries, can lead to higher wages over time.

Apart from FTZ's benefits to their host country at both a local and national level, there may also be economic exposure to criminal activities as a result of insufficient regulation. Research shows that the number of FTZs in an economy appears correlated with the value of exports of counterfeit and pirated products.

With less oversight, rogue actors are attracted to FTZs to engage in illegal and criminal trade. The OECD's findings indicate that one additional FTZ within an economy increases counterfeiting by 5.9 percent on average. It also appears that FTZs tend to be overly permissive by letting companies get away with poor safety and health conditions. This limited oversight is particularly troubling when one considers the potential for exploitation in areas such as human trafficking.

The OECD and EUIPO both stress the need for future action to curb the misuse of FTZs. They recommend developing clear guidelines for countries to increase transparency and promote clean and fair trade in FTZs, based on the involvement of industry members and key stakeholders of the trade supply chain.

The organizations identify three areas for future analysis. The first is the measurement of the role of FTZs in the trade of illicit and counterfeit goods. The next step requires a fuller quantitative analysis of counterfeit goods. Finally, further research needs to explore why counterfeit profiles differ from similar economies.

FTZs provide a number of advantages to economies, but without further regulation and research, they may induce heightened criminal activity. Both public and private actors must devise and apply strong deterrents to the establishment of criminal networks.

Together for More and Better

On a recent holiday, I had six teeth extracted. The insights I gathered during this process seemed relevant to current policy and election travails. My dentist's office was closed, but he kindly came in to see me. Of course, his staff did not, since it was a holiday, but that did not worry me since I wanted my doctor's skills, not those of his staff. After a lengthy procedure, my dentist gave me a pain prescription. Kind reader, please keep in mind—our local jurisdictions consist of the District of Columbia, the Commonwealth of Virginia, and the State of Maryland. Each state has different pharmaceutical rules and laws, and political leadership.

My dentist resides in Washington, DC; I live in Virginia, but have to drive through Maryland to get home. My daughter kindly offered to pick me up from the appointment, and as my pain was growing, we stopped at a pharmacy to purchase the medication on the way home. But with little luck. "We don't supply this medication," we were told. Little matter, we drove to the next pharmacy a few miles away in Maryland, where my daughter trains to be an emergency medical technician. But since the prescription was in my name, and I am a Virginian, we again obtained no medication, but growing pain from my teeth.

Onward then to Virginia. Yet, here I was informed that the pain medication was a narcotic, which in Virginia needed to be personally signed by the issuing doctor who, due to the holiday, had long ago left his office. Back to the car, with surging pain, we aimed for my home pharmacy where they know me. I always admonish my daughter to drive cautiously, but now I asked her to drive as fast as possible. It took 45 minutes, but finally, the home village came into sight. About one kilometer before the town, we heard a horn behind us and saw a blue emergency light. It was a visiting state trooper who stopped us for driving at an excessive speed. I started to explain, but his gestures made me quickly recall the saying of "tell it to the judge." Besides, I just wanted to get to the pharmacy.

The trooper was quite meticulous, but 40 minutes later, we were on the road again. At the pharmacy, we were immediately recognized and the prescription was, of course, filled right away. Apparently, word had gotten around regarding my earlier visits to other pharmacies since the pharmacist told me in confidence that "next time, just come here directly." The pills worked, and I thanked my daughter for her help, also promising to pay for all her expenses. In the end, the bills for speeding, lawyers, court cost, regular fees, speed measurement all added up to more than $1,300.

All this is truly not earth-shattering, but of major impact nonetheless. Lack of collaboration may start out by discomforting life, but given time and repetition, can lead to growing social gaps. America has, for more than one and a half centuries, principally drawn strength and a good life through success from its cohesiveness. Nevertheless, there have been shortcomings, apathies, and neglect, which require repair.

We must recognize and adjust our lives to cope with the growing complexity of the world today. Breaking up links and relationships is a bad idea. We continue to have an unsurpassed capacity for communication and analysis. We can find ways that allow for curative marketing or restitution for past or current wrongdoings. There clearly is room for improvement, be it for pain pills, jurisdiction, or treatment of people. Let's take steps for the pursuit of happiness, which supports us all. The Declaration of Independence has made a promise, but we as individuals need to deliver on it.

Sources

Chapter 1: International Connectedness

"The International Dream," *The Korea Times*, February 2019.

"Let Us Organize World Trade," *Michael Czinkota Blog*, February 2019.

"International Managers Have Choices," *OVI Magazine*, September 2018.

"The Unspoken Truth about International Business," *Michael Czinkota Blog*, July 2018.

"Global Medical Tourism," *Michael Czinkota Blog*, April 2018.

"A World without international marketing?" *Michael Czinkota Blog*, February 2018.

"Offsets: One answer to International Trade Imbalances," *Michael Czinkota Blog*, May 2018.

"The Secret to Trade Policy Success," *CEOWORLD Magazine*, September 2019

"Socialism Slows Progress," *OVI Magazine*, August 2019.

"Action and Imagery in the Middle East May Be Worth It," *Financial Mirror*, January 2020.

Chapter 2: Cultures in Play

"Spargelzeit," Voice of Vienna, *Ovi Magazine*, June 2020.

"Commonality Builds a Bridge," *Michael Czinkota Blog*, April 2019.

"Fish and Chips, All the Time?" *The Korea Times*, December 2018.

"In the Interest of Food," *Michael Czinkota Blog*, November 2018.

"No Hostilities Yet," *Michael Czinkota Blog*, October 2018.

"Olympics VS Super Bowl. The Marketing Differences," *The Korea Times*, February 2018.

"The Spring Break," *Michael Czinkota Blog*, March 2018.

"For Want of a Plane," *OVI Magazine*, December 2018.

"The Bear without the Bull," *Washington Examiner*, December 2019.

Chapter 3: Relationships With New Technology

"Technology: a Key Catalyst in a Changing Society," *Japan Today, Ovi Magazine, New Straits Times*, October 2020.

"America, Germany, and Hungary: A New Relationship," *Sri Lanka Guardian*, June 2020.

"Dealing with Disruptive Dislocations," *Voice of Vienna*, May 2020.

"International Data Need to Add Up," *New Straits Times*, April 2020.

"Services: Performance of the Future," *The Korea Times*, May 2019.

"History does not always tell the Future," *Michael Czinkota* Blog, March 2019.

"Fostering a new era of prosperity for US-EU relationship," *The Hill*, July 2018.

"The Case for Cuban Engagement," *OVI Magazine*, June 2018.

"Douse The Wildfires," *The Korea Times*, March 2019.

"The Ignorant Wise Man," *Sri* Lanka *Guardian*, January 2019.

"Package from China: Who pays the freight?" *The Daily Caller*, November 2018.

Chapter 4: Curative Marketing Can Cure

"Battling the Virus Strengthens Education," (with Michael L. Czinkota), *Shanghai Daily*, March 2020.

"The Coronavirus: A New Risk for Trade," *The Jerusalem Post*, February 2020.

"Good Souls Bring Curative Marketing," *The Korea Times*, April 2019.

"Free Trade Zones and Counterfeit Goods," *The Korea Times*, April 2018.

"Together for More and Better," *Michael Czinkota Blog*, 2020.

About the Author

Professor Michael Czinkota works on international marketing and trade at the McDonough School of Business of Georgetown University in Washington, DC and the University of Kent in Canterbury, United Kingdom. He is also the chaired professor emeritus for international marketing at the University of Birmingham in the United Kingdom. Fluent in English, Spanish, and German, he has held professorial appointments in Asia, Australia, Europe, and the Americas.

Dr. Czinkota served in the U.S. government administrations of Presidents Ronald Reagan and George H. W. Bush. As deputy assistant secretary at the Department of Commerce he was responsible for trade and investment analysis and reports, the CFIUS (Committee on Foreign Investment in the United States) and economic retaliatory actions. He also served as head of the U.S. delegation to the OECD (Organization for Economic Cooperation and Development) Industry Committee in Paris. In the Bureau of Export Administration, he was senior adviser for Export Controls.

Dr. Czinkota was a partner in a fur trading firm and in an advertising agency. His academic work has focused on export development strategies and the linkage between terrorism and international business. He is well-known for his 25 years' of Delphi Method studies, with participation by policy makers, business executives, and researchers from nations around the globe, to forecast international business change. He has written more than 137 articles in leading journals on the topics and was named one of the top three contributors to the international business literature by the *Journal of International Business.* In 2019, the Academy of International Business awarded him the Medal for Research Leadership in the past 50 years. Owing to his academic engagement on terrorism, Dr. Czinkota has worked with the U.S. Department of State and has testified more than 10 times before Congress.

He has authored 37 books in the fields of business, marketing, and trade. He also wrote three leading college textbooks, *International*

Marketing—10th edition, *International Business*—8th edition, and *Fundamentals of International Business*—3rd edition.

Dr. Czinkota served on the Global Advisory Board of the American Marketing Association, the Global Council of the American Management Association, the Board of Governors of the Academy of Marketing Science, and as a member of the American Council on Germany. For his work in international business and trade policy, he has been awarded honorary degrees by the Universidad del Pacífico in Lima, Peru, and the Universidad Pontificia Madre y Maestra in the Dominican Republic. The Universidad Ricardo Palma of Lima named its Global Marketing School after Dr. Czinkota.

He was named a Distinguished Fellow of the Academy of Marketing Science and a Fellow of the Royal Society of Arts in the United Kingdom. Dr. Czinkota serves on several corporate boards and has worked with corporations such as AT&T, IBM, GE, Nestle, and US WEST. He has advised the Executive Office of the President and the U.S. General Accountability Office on trade policy issues. He also serves as an advisor to the United Nations and the World Trade Organization. Dr. Czinkota was born and raised in Germany and educated in Austria, Scotland, Spain, and the United States. He studied law and business administration at the University of Erlangen-Nürnberg and was awarded a two-year Fulbright Scholarship. He holds an MBA in International Business and a PhD in Logistics from The Ohio State University.

Email: czinkotm@georgetown.edu
Phone Number: +1 (202) 253 3566
Blog: http://michaelczinkota.com/
LinkedIn: www.linkedin.com/in/michaelczinkota/

Selected Books from Michael R. Czinkota

Leading Textbooks for universities in United States, India, and Latin America:

International Marketing, 11th edition (with Ronkainen and Cui); CENGAGE Publishing 2021

International Business, 9th edition (with Ronkainen, Gupta); Cambridge University Press 2021

Marketing Management, 4th edition (with Kotabe, Vrontis, and Shams) 2021

Other Books with Business Expert Press:

In Search of the Soul of International Business, 2018

As I See It … Observations on International Business and Trade, 2017

As I was Thinking: Observations and Thoughts on International Business and Trade, 2014

As the World Turns … Observations on International Business and Policy, Going International and Transitions, 2012

As I Was Saying: Observations on International Business and Trade Policy, Exports, Education, and the Future, 2012

Emerging Trends, Threats and Opportunities in International Marketing: What Executives Need to Know, with Ilkka Ronkainen and Masaaki Kotabe, 2010

Index

OTHER TITLES IN THE INTERNATIONAL BUSINESS COLLECTION

S. Tamer Cavusgil, Manchester Business School;
Michael Czinkota, Georgetown; and
Gary Knight, Willamette University, Editors

- *Global Trends and Transformations in Culture, Business, and Technology* by Hamid Yeganeh
- *Adjusting to the New World Economy* by Michael Czinkota
- *The Chinese Market Series* by Danai Krokou
- *Trading With China* by Danai Krokou
- *The Chinese e-Merging Market* by Danai Krokou
- *The Chinese Market* by Danai Krokou
- *Creative Solutions to Global Business Negotiations, Third Edition* by Claude Cellich
- *Exporting* by Laurent Houlier and John Blaskey
- *Global Trade Strategies* by Michel Borgeon and Claude Cellich
- *Doing Business in Germany* by Andra Riemhofer
- *Major Business and Technology Trends Shaping the Contemporary World* by Hamid Yeganeh

Concise and Applied Business Books

The Collection listed above is one of 30 business subject collections that Business Expert Press has grown to make BEP a premiere publisher of print and digital books. Our concise and applied books are for...

- Professionals and Practitioners
- Faculty who adopt our books for courses
- Librarians who know that BEP's Digital Libraries are a unique way to offer students ebooks to download, not restricted with any digital rights management
- Executive Training Course Leaders
- Business Seminar Organizers

Business Expert Press books are for anyone who needs to dig deeper on business ideas, goals, and solutions to everyday problems. Whether one print book, one ebook, or buying a digital library of 110 ebooks, we remain the affordable and smart way to be business smart. For more information, please visit www.businessexpertpress.com, or contact sales@businessexpertpress.com.

www.ingramcontent.com/pod-product-compliance
Lightning Source LLC
Chambersburg PA
CBHW061837220326
41599CB00027B/5312